NuWave Oven Cookbook

Easy & Healthy NuWave Oven Recipes for the Everyday Home – Delicious Triple-Tested, Family-Approved NuWave Oven Recipes

… # © Copyright 2017 - All rights reserved.

The contents of this book may not be reproduced, duplicated or transmitted without direct written permission from the author.

Under no circumstances will any legal responsibility or blame be held against the publisher for any reparation, damages, or monetary loss due to the information herein, either directly or indirectly.

Legal Notice:
This book is copyright protected. This is only for personal use. You cannot amend, distribute, sell, use, quote or paraphrase any part or the content within this book without the consent of the author.

Disclaimer Notice:
Please note the information contained within this document is for educational and entertainment purposes only. Every attempt has been made to provide accurate, up to date and reliable complete information. No warranties of any kind are expressed or implied. Readers acknowledge that the author is not engaging in the rendering of legal, financial, medical or professional advice. The content of this book has been derived from various sources. Please consult a licensed professional before attempting any techniques outlined in this book.

By reading this document, the reader agrees that under no circumstances are is the author responsible for any losses, direct or indirect, which are incurred as a result of the use of information contained within this document, including, but not limited to, — errors, omissions, or inaccuracies.

Table of Contents

Introduction	8
Chapter 1: Advantages of Cooking With the NuWave Oven	9
Time Saver	*9*
Meats & Fish Turn Out Absolutely Delicious	*9*
Healthy Cooking	*10*
Energy Saver	*10*
Reheat Like a Pro	*11*
Chapter 2: Tips & Tricks for Cooking With the NuWave Oven	12
Chapter 3: FAQ's	14
Chapter 4: Parts and Design	25
Chapter 5: NuWave Oven Temperature Conversion Guide	29
Tips for Recipe Conversion	*29*
General Cooking Conversion Guide (From the Internet)	30
Chapter 6: NuWave Oven Specific Recipes	31
Breakfast Recipes	*31*
Delicious Cinnamon Breakfast Twists	31
Delicious Mushroom, Ham & Spinach Quiche	32
Oven Omelets	33
NuWave Style Cheesy English Muffin Sandwich	34
Crunchy Low Calorie French Toast	35
Steak, Eggs & Cheese Stuffed Tomatoes	36
Delicious Ham and Cheese Strata	37
Ham & Eggs Scramble	38
Deliciously Cheesy Asparagus Frittatas	39

English Muffin and Egg Casserole	41
Potato and Pork Breakfast Bake	42
Brunch Bread Pudding	43
Delicious Blueberry and Pecan Streusel Cake	45
Mini Crustless Quiche	47
Appetizers	*48*
Delicious Cereal Party Mix	48
Sour Cream and Ranch Stuff Potato Bites	49
Bacon Wrapped Shrimp Bites	50
Toasted Bacon, Apple and Grilled Cheese Sandwiches	51
Goat Cheese, Pear and Walnut Crostini	52
Cheesy Mixed Vegetable Quesadillas	53
Loaded NuWave Nachos	54
Delicious 3 Cheese Garlic Bread	55
Delicious Cheddar, Jalapeño & Corn Muffins	56
Cheesy Garlic Buttermilk Biscuit Bread Bites	57
Baked Herb Cheese Fries	59
Italian Bread Loaf Pizza	61
Cheese Burst Bacon Wrapped Tater Tots	62
Delicious Chicken in Alfredo Sauce Roll Ups	63
Poultry Recipes	*65*
Crispy Ginger and Honey Crusted Chicken	65
Delicious Whole Italian Style Chicken	66
Sweet & Spicy Barbeque Chicken	67
Spinach, Ham & Sun Dried Tomatoes Stuffed Chicken Roulade	68
Roasted Dijon and Herb Encrusted Chicken Breast	69

Chicken Parmesan	70
Sour Cream Topped Chicken Breasts with Mushrooms & Bell Peppers	71
Delicious Chicken Bites with a Wasabi Mayonnaise Dipping Sauce	72
Quick & Easy Barbeque Chicken	74
Hot & Spicy Buffalo Chicken Hoagie Roll Sandwiches	75
Oven Fried Chicken	76
Grilled Cornish Game Hens with Artichokes & Potatoes	78
Grilled Garlic & Cilantro Chicken Breasts	79
Delicious Chicken Curry	80
Pork Recipes	*81*
Asian Style Pork Chops with a Tangy Pineapple Relish	81
Baked Ham in Cola	82
Thai Style Grilled Pork Tenderloin	83
Delicious Casserole with Sausage, Rice & Vegetables	84
Juicy Pork Shoulder	85
Delicious Apple & Onion Stuffed Pork Roulade	87
Andouille Sausage Burgers with a Spicy Mayonnaise	88
Hot and Spicy Chorizo Burgers	90
Sweet and Spicy Baby Back Ribs	92
Brine Soaked And Bacon Covered Grilled Pork Loin	93
Tangy Orange Marmalade Glazed Spareribs	95
Hot and Spicy Pork Chops	96
Fennel and Anise Seed Crusted Pork Loin	97
Delicious Rum Soaked Pork Chops	98
Beef and Lamb Recipes	*99*
Quick and Easy Rib Roast	99

Speedy Lamb Meatballs	100
Delicious and Cheesy Beef Burgers	101
Delicious Ancho Chili Spiced Lamb Burgers	102
Yankee Style Pot Roast	104
Lamb Chops with a Mint and Red Pepper Sauce	105
Delicious Andouille & Beef Burgers with Spicy Mayonnaise and Caramelized Onions	106
Feta and Tomato Topped Grilled Lamb Chops	108
Spicy Louisiana Sliders with a Mustard Remoulade Sauce	109
Herb Butter Stuffed Lamb Chops	111
Delicious Beef Burger in Olive Bread Slices	112
Barbeque Lamb Skewers	114
Delicious Veggie and Meat Tortilla Rolls	115
Seafood Recipes	*116*
Tasty Tuna Noodle Casserole	116
A Medley of Shellfish	117
Tangy Lemon Salmon Topped With a Sweet and Spicy Mango Salsa	118
NuWave Style Quick N Easy Lobster Thermidor	119
Zingy Roasted Shrimp with a Herbed Salsa	120
Delicious Potato Topped Tilapia Fillets with A Herbed Sour Cream	121
Simple Tuna Steaks with a Tangy Orange Salsa	122
Spicy Red Snapper with Red Onion and Orange	123
Cheesy Crab Dip with Toasted Wonton Wrappers	124
Grilled Halibut with a Tangy Clementine Gremolata	126
Fennel Coated Bass	127
Hot & Zingy Clams & Sausage	128
Vegetables Recipes	*129*

Delicious Mayonnaise & Cheese Covered Corn	129
Almond Topped Crunchy French Beans	130
Cheesy Zucchini and Onion Au Gratin	131
Parmesan Crusted Asparagus Spears with Balsamic Vinegar	132
Streusel Topped Buttery Sweet Potato Casserole	133
Delicious Feta and Artichoke Tortilla Wraps with a Chive and Yogurt Dip	134
Tofu, Cheese and Marinara Sauce Stuffed Bell Peppers	135
Spicy Grilled Vegetables with a Yogurt and Tahini Dip	136
Roasted Garlic Mushrooms	137
Roasted Cauliflower, Olives and Chickpeas	138
Quick and Easy Roasted Butternut Squash	139
Delicious Ricotta and Spinach Stuffer Lasagna Rolls	140
Desserts Recipes	*142*
Pumpkin Cookie Sandwiches with a Cream Cheese Filling	142
Delicious Dense Pound Cake	144
Delicious Chocolate Topped Oat Cookies	146
Lemon And Poppy Seed Glazed Cookies	148
Maraschino Cherry Stuffed Cherry Glazed Cookies	150
Lemon Candy Topped Iced Cookies	152
Salted Chocolate Tart	154
Conclusion	156

Introduction

Congratulations on your smart purchase of the NuWave Oven!

This highly popular multipurpose countertop appliance has the combination of three types of heat – convection, conduction and infrared. This unique combination saves a lot of energy and time, while cutting the extra fats and calories from your foods.

When you cook in a NuWave oven, you do not need to pre-heat it nor do you need to defrost food before placing it in the oven. Remove the frozen foods from the freezer and directly pop them into your NuWave oven. Set the time and temperature and sit back and relax while your NuWave oven does all the hard work!

The NuWave oven also uses a 'layered cooking' model for added convenience. This means that you can cook multiple items in your NuWave oven at the same time, without their flavors mixing up or mingling together. So, you can prepare a vegetarian dish and a non-vegetarian dish together, without any of the flavors spoiling the taste of the separated dishes.

When you prepare food in your NuWave oven, you are making a healthy choice. This is because you do not need to use any extra fat while cooking in a NuWave oven. That's right; no extra butter or oil needed to do any of the cooking. Also, if you are using fat rich meats or your marinade has a healthy amount of fat in it, do not worry! The unique design of the NuWave oven ensures that all the excess fat from your food is drained and all you get it succulent and delicious low fat food! Because of its three heat technology, vegetables not only cook faster, but also retain a great deal of the nutritional value present in them that is usually lost when you cook vegetables in a regular oven!

In this book, you will find every bit of information that you need for the proper functioning of your NuWave oven. From the advantages of using a NuWave oven, tips and tricks for quicker and better cooking, FAQs, a brief on all the components and buttons present on the oven, temperature conversions, a handy kitchen conversion guide and a bunch of NuWave recipes, this book has it all!

I would like to take this opportunity to thank you for purchasing this book and I hope you find the content of this book enlightening and useful!

Chapter 1: Advantages of Cooking With the NuWave Oven

To put it simply, the NuWave Oven is a new way of cooking. This oven uses three different systems of heat production together, namely convection, infrared and conduction in order to cook food more efficiently.

Here are some of the advantages of using a NuWave Oven:

Time Saver
In today's fast paced world, no one has the time to slave in the kitchen for hours. We all need equipment that will produce great tasting food in a short time and with minimum effort needed.

One of the biggest advantages of the NuWave oven is that it is a real time saver. You do not need to preheat it in advance. This saves you a good 20 minutes (that you would have spent waiting for your oven to reach the right temperature) and you can just turn the switch on, place your food in and it will be cooked in no time at all!

Another important time saver is that by cooking frozen foods all the way through, they don't have to be defrosted first. Yes, you read that right. You no longer need to defrost your frozen foods to room temperature before you cook them. Extract your frozen food from the freezer, place in your NuWave oven, set the temperature and voila your delicious food will be ready in no time at all!

The NuWave oven, as mentioned before, cooks food faster. Users have noticed that they have been able to shave off a good 5 to 20 minutes of cooking time (depending upon the food item they were cooking).

Meats & Fish Turn Out Absolutely Delicious
You can cook a variety of foods in the NuWave oven, from vegetables to poultry to meat to seafood of all kinds, but regular users agree that the best use for your NuWave oven is to cook some delicious meat or fish in it.

Poultry such as turkey and chicken can be cooked whole or in parts and it turns out deliciously tender and juicy with a perfectly golden brown exterior. Fatty meats, such as pork or lamb cook beautifully in the oven, having the perfect balance of fatty tenderness and juiciness in them. Fish cooked in the NuWave oven has a perfectly flaky interior combined with a crisp exterior.

You can achieve perfectly cooked meats in the NuWave oven, without having to constantly check them or constantly baste them!

Healthy Cooking

Today, everybody is diet conscious and nobody wants to consume unhealthy food that is drenched in fat. Cooking food without fat or with very little fat usually results in chewy dried out food with no juiciness to it. In such a scenario, the NuWave oven will be your new best friend!

The NuWave oven, as explained before, uses a triple combo cooking power to cook foods. This dynamic cooking method extracts all the excess fat from the food, in the form of fat drippings, while the food remains juicy and tender on the inside.

Also, with a quicker cooking cycle, the NuWave oven ensures that the nutritional value in your food is not lost due to heating for many hours.

So, at the end of the day, you have delicious food on your plate that is low on fat, but is extremely juicy and has most of its nutrients intact!

Energy Saver

When you use the NuWave oven, not only are you saving time and making yourself some delicious food, but you are also doing your bit to save the planet. How? Read on to learn! Using the NuWave oven instead of your regular oven saves you a lot of energy. A whopping 2/3 of the energy that you would usually be used to work your conventional oven is used by the NuWave oven. This is because you do not waste any energy preheating your oven. When you use a conventional oven, you need to preheat it, in order for it to achieve the ideal temperature. This uses a lot of energy.

The NuWave oven is a small compact unit and all the heat generated by it is centralized. So, it does not take a lot of energy for it to achieve ideal cooking temperature. Another advantage of using the NuWave oven is that it does not increase the average temperature of your kitchen while in use. While in warm weather, this is a blessing because it does not conflict with the air conditioning!

Reheat Like a Pro
The worst part about leftovers is reheating – the food never seems to recover from is trip to the fridge and loses all its firmness after reheating. What if I tell you that the NuWave oven will not just reheat your food, but breathe a new life into it? Imagine, reheating a pizza without its crust getting hard and the whole pizza getting chewy. Sounds like heaven doesn't it?

Re-heat some refrigerated fried chicken leftovers and watch as its excess fat drips away, leaving you with a fat free and crispy chicken for you to eat and enjoy!

Chapter 2: Tips & Tricks for Cooking With the NuWave Oven

Here is a list of some handy trips and tricks that will help you cook in and clean your NuWave oven in a quicker and timelier manner!

- Using the multi-level cooking feature on the NuWave oven is both fun and extremely easy! All you need to remember is that all the foods do not take the same time to get perfectly cooked. So, the foods that take longer to cook, such as meats, should be placed in the oven on the lower racks and once they are almost done, faster cooking foods should be placed on the higher racks.

- On a similar note, while preparing stews, chowders, soups or gumbos, you should let the broth simmer and add in the ingredients in according to their cooking times to ensure proper cooking.

- Did you know that you can not only bake and grill in your NuWave oven, but can also toast a variety of breads, bagels or English muffins in it? Place your choice of bread on a 4-inch rack on high and you will have perfectly toasted bread in about 4 minutes.

- After grilling your favorite meats, cleaning up the fat droppings can be an absolute pain. To help you clean up easier and headache free, place a piece of heavy-duty aluminum foil on the Linear Pan. After you are done cooking, you can just lift the foil off the Linear Pan and get rid of it (along with all the mess), without having to scrub the pan!

- Whenever you handle your NuWave oven, during or after cooking, ensure that you always have your oven mitts on. You may not feel the heat radiating off it immediately, but your NuWave oven is hot and can scald your palms and fingers terribly if you are not careful!

- It is essential that you clean your NuWave oven after each use. If you do not clean after each use, the leftovers from your previous cook may end up burning and sticking to your oven, making the clean up afterwards an even bigger head ache!

- Every time you clean your NuWave oven, ensure that the oven is turned off, cooled and unplugged before you begin.

- Before removing the power head from your NuWave oven, ensure that the dome of the oven has cooled sufficiently and fan has stopped working.

- Do not, I repeat do not, place the power head in the dishwasher or under running water or dunk it in water. Only the exterior of the power head should be cleaned using a lightly damp cloth.

- Avoid using rough pads or chemical cleaners while cleaning your NuWave oven. They will damage the surface of your oven. It is also advisable that you do not put any of the enamel racks in the dishwasher and you should always wash them by hand whenever possible.

Chapter 3: FAQ's

1. What is the meaning of TCC (Triple Combo Cooking) power?

The TCC system can be defined to be a combination of three different cooking methods:

- **Conduction**: Conduction is when heat from the source is directly applied to the food.

- **Convection:** Convection is when heat is applied indirectly to the food. In this case, hot air is produced by a motor and circulated through the oven using a specially designed fan. This results in even cooking and browning. It also locks the moisture in the food, resulting in juicy and tender food!

- **Infrared:** Infrared heat is an invisible, gentle and radiant form of heat that not only cooks the food from the outside, but also penetrates into the food to ensure even cooking and adequate moisture retention. The concept of infrared heat can be compared to the heat of the sun's rays that reflect on our skin.

2. What is the basic difference between a Halogen Oven and an Infrared Oven?

- To put it basically, halogen ovens use 1200-watt halogen bulbs as the main source of heat, whereas an infrared NuWave oven uses a 1500-watt sheath heater as the main source of heat.

- Another difference between most halogen ovens and the infrared NuWave oven is that halogen ovens usually have a glass base tray and a glass dome, while the infrared NuWave oven has a highly durable plastic dome. While glass domes may quickly heat up while cooking and may break quite easily, plastic domes do not get heated up as easily and also have a higher level of durability.

- Also, halogen ovens can only be used for an hour at a stretch and need to be cooled down before further use. As opposed to this, the NuWave infrared oven can be used for close to 10 hours at a stretch on low power level, while it can be used for close to 2 hours at a stretch on the max temperature level.

- The glass dome in a halogen oven needs to be scrubbed and washed properly, or else the food you are trying to cook in it will not cook evenly. This is because of the reflection of heat in the glass dome and the heat will not be able to transfer properly from the halogen bulb to the food in the oven. This will result in food that is burned on the bottom, while raw on the top! The NuWave oven's special TCC power ensures that your food is cooked evenly and uniformly always.

- Halogen ovens weigh close to about 20 pounds, while the infrared NuWave oven weighs only 9 pounds.

Here are some basic differences between a regular halogen oven and the infrared NuWave oven.

3. How is infrared an aid for cooking?

Infrared energy is made up of the energy frequencies that can be found just beneath the red side of the spectrum that is usually visible. These frequencies have a unique effect on organic molecules – when these frequencies interact with organic molecules, they cause them to vibrate at a high speed, thus producing heat from within.

Although it should be observed that almost any type of electromagnetic energy could be used for the purpose of heating and cooking, infrared energy is the best choice for it as it cooks food evenly and quickly, as compared to the other sources of energy.

4. Even after changing my power level to 10, my NuWave oven takes close to 3 hours to cook a chicken breast. Why does this happen?

- The oven will, by design, default to the HI power level.

- When you press the power level and select the option of '1', the display console will display a power level of '10'. But, this just means that your oven is set to 10% of the total heating power, i.e., just 10% of 350 degrees F.

- So, whenever you are setting the power levels, it is extremely important that you adjust the power levels according to the manual or else you will end up cooking food at a lower temperature for a longer period of time.

5. Where can I find the serial number and the model number of my NuWave oven?

- The serial number and the model number can be found at the back of the power head of the oven.

- The serial number is usually in alphabet form followed by a bunch of numbers.

6. According to the manual, my NuWave oven can bake, barbeque, dehydrate, air fry, broil, roast, grill and steam. How do I use all these functions in my NuWave oven? Is there a button I need to press to switch functions?

To put it simply, yes you can do all the aforementioned functions and a lot more in your NuWave oven. All you need to do is prep your food according to the function you wish to use. Here is how to prep food according to the cooking method you wish to use.

- To air fry: Dip your food in a wet batter and then roll it in bread crumbs, cornflakes or some rolled oats. Spray some cooking spray or brush on some olive oil if you want your food to be a little extra brown. If you wish to reheat fried foods, just spray with some cooking spray – they will come out a lot crispier than before.

- To steam: Cover your food with some heavy-duty aluminum foil, add in a little water and seasoning.

- To broil: Place your food closer to the heat source.

- To roast: Place your food away from the heat source and cook on a low power level.

- To dehydrate: Cook your food on a lower power level and once the food is done, remove it immediately from the oven before it can absorb any moisture.

7. Can I cook a turkey without using an extender ring?

- You can cook a turkey that weighs up to 10 lbs. in your NuWave oven without using an extender ring.

- By using an extender ring you increase the capacity of your NuWave oven by close to 50% and can easily cook a 16 lb. turkey in your NuWave oven without any fuss!

8. How can I remove the frozen turkey giblets? And what if I wish to stuff my turkey with a filling?

- When you start cooking your turkey, it is advisable that you cook it with its breast side down during the first half of the cooking time.

- When you turn the turkey over at the halfway mark to turn it breast side up, the inside of the turkey should be softened enough so that you can easily remove the giblets from it.

- If you wish to stuff your turkey, there are two ways in which this can be done:

    o It is advisable that you add the stuffing during the last 45 minutes of your cooking time.

- o If you are unavailable to stuff the turkey during the last 45 minutes, stuff the turkey from the beginning and add about 3 extra minutes per pound of turkey to the total cooking time.

9. How do you add seasoning to frozen food?

There are a few ways in which you can easily season frozen foods:

- If you wish to add dry seasoning, such as oregano, chili flakes, basil, salt, pepper, etc. to your frozen food, first sprinkle a little water over your food before adding the seasoning. This ensures that the seasoning "sticks" to your food.

- If you are using wet seasoning, such as barbeque sauce, mushroom sauce, etc., pour it over the frozen food. When you flip your food over, make sure you add more of your sauce onto the food to ensure even seasoning.

- If you are freezing your own meats, fish or vegetables, it is advisable that you marinate them or sprinkle the seasoning of your choice over them before storing them in the freezer.

10. Do I need to flip the food over?

- It is highly recommended that you flip over the food about halfway through the cooking process. This is not for even cooking, but for even browning and better presentation.

- This is because the heat source is situated at the top of the oven. So even though the infrared method ensures that your food is cooked through even without flipping, the conductive method, which is responsible for the browning, cannot reach the bottom of the food.

- If you do not flip your food, the top will be browned, while the bottom, even though cooked through, will look raw and unappealing.

11. Is it easy and fuss free to clean the NuWave oven after use?

- Cleaning up a NuWave oven is a breeze.

- All parts of the NuWave oven can be separated quite easily for cleaning.

- All parts of the NuWave oven, apart from the power head, are completely dishwasher safe.

- To ensure that your dome lasts longer and doesn't spoil easily, it is advisable that you clean it immediately after use.

- While washing the parts of the NuWave oven in the dishwasher, you do not need to use the heated dry cycle feature. This ensures that you save on your energy costs too!

12. The area I live in has a perpetual warm climate. Will the NuWave oven add to the heat by heating up my kitchen?

- With NuWave's Triple Combo Cooking feature, you do not need to preheat your oven or defrost your frozen foods.

- The NuWave oven dos not heat up your kitchen while in use as it doesn't heat up the surrounding air. This makes it the ideal appliance to use in a small confined place, during hot summers and even in places that have an extremely hot climate.

- The NuWave oven uses about 15% of the energy that is used by a normal conventional oven. Your NuWave oven not only saves you energy and time, but it also has absolutely no effect on the temperature of your kitchen.

13. Are there specific types of pans that I need to use in my NuWave oven?

- Any types of cooking utensils that can be used in a conventional oven are safe to use in your NuWave oven.

- This means that you can easily use equipment or utensils that are made of foil, Pyrex, metals, prepared frozen entrée trays and oven safe cooking bags in your NuWave oven.

- The basic rule of thumb is that if it can be used in a regular conventional oven, it can be used in your NuWave oven.

14. Can multiple food items be cooked in the NuWave oven simultaneously? Is it big enough to place multiple food items at once?

- The Triple Combo Cooking method used by the NuWave oven ensures that you can cook multiple food items in the oven at the same time.

- To put it simply, it takes the NuWave oven about 50 minutes to cook a Cornish hen. Even if you were to place 4 Cornish hens together in your NuWave oven, the cooking time will not increase to 3 hours; it will still remain 50 minutes.

- As for being big enough, the NuWave can easily accommodate about 3 different layers of food items easily.

15. Can vegetarian dishes be cooked in the NuWave oven? Do they cook properly? How can you cook vegetables in different ways?

Preparing vegetables or vegetarian dishes in the NuWave oven is extremely easy. It is also very advantageous because the triple cooking combo power of the NuWave ensures that there is a minimal loss of nutrients from the vegetables, nutrients that are easily lost when cooking with other methods. Using little amount of water and subjecting the vegetables to a smaller cooking time add to the effectiveness of this oven.

Here is how to prepare vegetables using different methods:

- To roast: place the vegetables directly onto the 4-inch rack.

- To steam: loosely wrap the vegetables in aluminum foil and sprinkle a small amount of water on them to ensure that there is a proper circulation of steam in the oven.

- To steam vegetables and give them a roasted flavor: take the aluminum foil out during the last two minutes of the cooking process and roast the vegetables directly.

Preparing a variety of vegetables and vegetarian dishes is quite simple and easy in the NuWave oven. Here are some simple and handy tips to keep in mind when you cook vegetables in your NuWave oven:

- For a quick and easy snack, brush some asparagus with a little olive oil and roast for about 8 minutes. Perfectly cooked delicious asparagus is ready to eat!

- To prepare sweet or baked potatoes, wash them thoroughly, poke them with a fork and season with oil or butter combined with seasoning of your choice. Place on the rack and cook on the highest setting for about 45 minutes, flipping the potatoes over at the halfway mark. Healthy baked potatoes are ready to eat!

- You do not need to use extra fats, such as oil or butter, to prepare most vegetables. Simply toss them in some dressing of your choice and roast them for a delicious flavor.

- If you feel that your vegetables are browning too quickly, just cover them with an aluminum foil. Your vegetables will not burn before the cooking process is over.

16. Is there a creation of smoke in the NuWave oven?

- Thanks to the Triple Combo Cooking Power, a synergy is created in the NuWave oven. Also, with the Triple Cooking Combo power, food cooks faster while being subjected to a lower amount of heat. Because of the combination of these two features, smoke generation is at a bare minimum.

- Due to its superior design, the NuWave oven confines all the smoke that is generated in the oven and negates the need for ventilation in the kitchen.

17. What is the highest temperature that the NuWave oven can generate?

- The NuWave oven has a total of 10 different power settings. The 'HI' setting is the maximum setting of the oven.

- On the 'HI' setting the maximum temperature achieved is an approximate 350 degrees F. (to see how power levels correspond with temperature levels, refer to the temperature conversion chart in a later chapter of this book)

- Due to its highly efficient Triple Combo Cooking power, the NuWave oven cooks food at a quicker rate than the normal conventional oven. For example, it takes the NuWave oven about 2 and half hours to cook a frozen solid 10 lb. turkey to perfection.

18. While using the NuWave oven, how much energy and time can one save?

- While regular conventional ovens use about 3400 watts of energy, the NuWave oven uses a mere 1500 watts; less than half of the energy usually used!

- As mentioned before, with the NuWave oven, you do not need to defrost frozen foods or preheat the oven before cooking. Because of this feature, the NuWave oven not only uses about 15% of the energy usually used by conventional ovens, but also cooks food about 50% faster than normal.

19. When referring to recipes or charts, what is meant by the 1-inch rack or 4-inch rack?

- The cooking rack can be used on both sides, giving you both a 1-inch height as well as a 4-inch height.

- The 4-inch rack is ideal to cook smaller foods in, such as vegetables, shrimp or chicken breasts.

- The 1-inch rack is ideal to cook larger foods in, such as a whole stuffed chicken, a large steak or a 10 lb. turkey.

20. For how long has the NuWave range of ovens been available in the market?

- Hearthware, the company behind NuWave, has been in the countertop infrared oven manufacturing business since 1997.

- Hearthware is the original producer of the Infrared Cooking System.

21. What is the size of the NuWave oven and what are its exact dimensions?

- The NuWave oven weighs about 9 lbs.

- From the inside, the NuWave oven is about 12-inches in diameter and about 6.5-inches deep.

- From the outside, the NuWave oven is about 13.5-inches tall and about 15.5-inches wide.

- It can be plugged into a regular household outlet and has the cooking power of 1500 watts. It uses 12.5 amps.

22. While cooking multiple foods together in the NuWave oven, do the smells and tastes of the foods mix together?

No, none of the flavors or smells of the foods cooked in the NuWave oven mix together. Even if you are cooking fish on one level and vegetables on the other, the flavors or the smells of the foods will not get combined together.

23. What shipping services are used to ship the NuWave Oven?

The NuWave oven is shipped to customers via efficient and trusted shipping partners, FedEx, UPS or USPS.

The oven is packed using high quality protective packaging and weighs about 16 pounds when shipped.

Chapter 4: Parts and Design

The NuWave oven is a modern oven that uses the Triple Combo Cooking power to efficiently prepare food in less time and using less energy.

The main components of the NuWave oven are the liner pan, power head, base, reversible cooking rack and transparent dome cover. Also, there are analog control dials on the power head as well as a digital control panel. Additionally, you can get yourself a 3-inch extender ring to increase the cooking capacity of your NuWave oven and also get yourself a few ovenproof dishes (though you do not need to buy specific equipment, as any you can use any equipment that is safe to use in a conventional oven.)

In this chapter you will find a brief explanation on all the parts present in your NuWave oven and it also contains handy tips and tricks that you can use to maintain your NuWave oven.

The Base

The name is pretty self-explanatory. The base is the lowest part of the oven and holds the liner pan in it. The base is dishwasher safe, but you can easily place it under running warm water to clean it or you can clean it using a damp cloth too.

The base is one of the sturdiest parts of the NuWave oven and you will find that if you properly maintain it, you will never need to replace it. Although, if you need a replacement, you will find a replacement quite easily available. Just ensure the color matches the rest of your oven and you are good to go.

Depending upon the models available, three-color variations are available, namely white and blue, silver and black and white and red. The replacement cost for all color variations is the same.

Liner Pan

Designed to fit perfectly inside the base of the NuWave oven, the liner pan can hold a number of items in it, from drip trays, to casseroles to pans.

The liner pan is enameled and it is advisable that you do not place it in the dishwasher. The best way to keep the liner pan clean is by placing the liner pan under a stream of warm water or wiping it clean using a damp rag. Do not use high heat or abrasive chemicals to clean the liner pan or else the enamel layer will get damaged.

If maintained well, your liner pan will not need to be replaced. However, if you require a replacement, replacements are easily available. Just ensure that the new liner pan fits your NuWave oven.

Cooking Rack

This is the place where all your cooking magic takes place.

As already mentioned, one of the methods the NuWave oven uses to cook food is conduction. To explain it in a layman's language, conduction is when a hot thing touches the cold thing, making the cold thing hot. Here, the hot thing is the cooking rack and the cold thing is your food.

There are multiple racks available in the market such as, 2-inch, reversible 1 – 4-inch and mini rack. While the reversible rack comes with your purchase of the NuWave oven, the other two racks can be bought separately.

The cooking rack is dishwasher safe. It can also be washed by placing it under a stream of warm water or with a damp rag.

As for replacement, replacements are easily available in the market. Just ensure that the new rack fits in your NuWave oven.

Transparent Dome Cover

The transparent dome cover is one of the most important parts of the NuWave oven. Made using high quality plastic and not tempered glass, the transparent dome cover is highly durable and almost unbreakable.

The transparent dome cover is dishwasher safe. It is highly advisable that you clean the transparent dome cover as soon as you are done with the cooking process. This is to ensure that food items do not stick to your transparent dome cover, making it difficult to clean.

Replacing the transparent dome cover is extremely easy as replacements are easily available in the market.

Power Head

The power head is the most important part of the NuWave oven. This is where the infrared rods, all the wiring, heating element, the little motor and the special fan are located. This part is absolutely not dishwasher safe and should not be subjected to water in any way possible. Instead, after every use, you need to wipe the power head with a lightly damp rag and then immediately wipe off the moisture using a dry cloth. Before doing so, unplug the oven.

The patented infrared rods present in the power head are responsible for the even cooking of food, on the inside as well as the outside. This cooking method also helps to trap the natural oils of the food that keep the food moist, while getting rid of the excess fat through fat drips.

The silent motor and the special fan are responsible for the even distribution of hot air through the oven, ensuring even cooking and higher moisture retention in food.

There are two types of power heads available – the analog power head and the digital power head. The analog power head has a bunch of knobs on the top while the digital power head has a digital display.

Digital Control Panel and Analog Control Dials

The digital control panel and analog control dials are a part of the power head. The digital control panel can control the power level, cooking time and the temperature with just a few presses of the button, while the analog power head has dials for the same function.

Extender Ring

An optional piece of equipment, the extender ring, is usually used to increase the capacity of a regular NuWave oven by a good 50%. It adds about 3-inches of space to your NuWave oven and can be used together with the cooking rack.

Chapter 5: NuWave Oven Temperature Conversion Guide

Oven Temperature	Power Level
116 degrees Fahrenheit (47 degrees Celsius)	1
106 degrees Fahrenheit (41 degrees Celsius)	2
150 degrees Fahrenheit (66 degrees Celsius)	3
175 degrees Fahrenheit (79 degrees Celsius)	4
225 degrees Fahrenheit (107 degrees Celsius)	5
250 degrees Fahrenheit (121 degrees Celsius)	6
275 degrees Fahrenheit (135 degrees Celsius)	7
300 degrees Fahrenheit (149 degrees Celsius)	8
325 degrees Fahrenheit (163 degrees Celsius)	9
342 degrees Fahrenheit (172 degrees Celsius)	10 (HI)

Tips for Recipe Conversion

- If the directions listed in the recipe call for temperatures higher than 350 degrees Fahrenheit, cook on the 'HI' setting for the time stated in the recipe for perfectly cooked dishes.

- If the directions listed in the recipe call for temperatures lower than 350 degrees Fahrenheit, cook at the required temperature setting for 25% less time than stated in the recipe for perfectly cooked dishes.

General Cooking Conversion Guide (From the Internet)

Volume Conversions	
Metric	**US**
5 mL	1 teaspoon
15 mL	1 tablespoon or 1/2 fluid ounce
30 mL	1 fluid ounce or 1/8 cup
60 mL	1/4 cup or 2 fluid ounces
80 mL	1/3 cup
120 mL	1/2 cup or 4 fluid ounces
160 mL	2/3 cup
180 mL	3/4 cup or 6 fluid ounces
240 mL	1 cup or 8 fluid ounces or half a pint
350 mL	1 1/2 cups or 12 fluid ounces
475 mL	2 cups or 1 pint or 16 fluid ounces
700 mL	3 cups or 1 1/2 pints
950 mL	4 cups or 2 pints or 1 quart
3.8 L	4 quarts or 1 gallon
28 grams	1 oz.
454 grams	1 pound
Weight Conversions	
Metric	**US**
28 g	1 ounce
113 g	4 ounces or 1/4 pound
150 g	1/3 pound
230 g	8 ounces or 1/2 pound
300 g	2/3 pound
340 g	12 ounces or 3/4 pound
450 g	1 pound or 16 ounces
900 g	2 pounds

Chapter 6: NuWave Oven Specific Recipes

Breakfast Recipes

Delicious Cinnamon Breakfast Twists

Serves: 2

Ingredients:
- 1 teaspoons cinnamon
- 1/2 cup sugar
- 1/2 (11-ounce) package frozen breadsticks

Directions:
1. Combine the cinnamon and sugar in a medium sized mixing bowl. Whisk together using a wire whisk until well combined. Set aside.
2. Pour the cinnamon sugar into a flat plate.
3. Place a single breadstick in the cinnamon sugar mixture and roll until well coated.
4. Hold the breadstick from both ends in each hand and twist until you get a rope like texture.
5. Place on a 3-inch rack and bake on 'HI' for about 12 to 14 minutes, flipping it over at the halfway mark.
6. Serve with a side of apple sliced.
7. Enjoy!

Tip:
1. If you want softer and chewy twists, bake for about 7 to 9 minutes.
2. You can also brush the done cinnamon twisty with some melted butter and sprinkle some more cinnamon sugar on the twisty for some added flavor.
3. For a savory option, brush the breadstick with some egg and top with grated cheese, sesame seeds or some poppy seeds.

Delicious Mushroom, Ham & Spinach Quiche

Ingredients:
- 1 egg
- 1/2 cup ham, diced
- 1/2 cup loosely packed spinach
- 2 large mushrooms, chopped
- 1/2 cup Swiss cheese, shredded
- 1/2 cup milk
- 1/4 cup Bisquick
- ¼ teaspoon pepper

Directions:
1. Place the spinach leaves, chopped mushrooms and diced ham in the bottom of a silicon liner, an oven safe dish or on a sheet of heavy-duty aluminum foil. Place it on a 3-inch rack.
2. Cook for about 8 to 10 minutes on the 'HI' setting.
3. While the mushroom, spinach and ham mix is cooking, place the egg in the medium sized mixing bowl.
4. Add in the milk, Bisquick and pepper and whisk well until combined.
5. Pour the prepared egg mixture into a 4-inch by 4-inch silicon baking dish. Add in the cooked ham, spinach and mushroom mix and mix well.
6. Sprinkle the shredded Swiss cheese on the top in a single layer.
7. Place the pan on the 1-inch rack and bake on the 'HI' setting for about 20 to 25 minutes or until a fork inserted in the center of the dish comes out clean.
8. Remove the dish from your NuWave oven and let it se for about 5 minutes before cutting into cubes and serving.
9. Serve hot with a side of toasted bagels and a glass of orange juice.
10. Enjoy!

Oven Omelets

Serves: 2

Ingredients:
- 5 eggs
- 3 ounces Cheddar cheese, shredded
- 1/4 cup milk
- 1/2 cup bacon or ham, chopped into bite sized pieces
- 1/8 cup onion, chopped
- 1/4 cup green pepper, chopped
- 1/2 tablespoon parsley

Directions:
1. Place the eggs in a medium sized mixing bowl. Add in the milk and beat using a whisk until the eggs get a fluffy texture.
2. Add in the cheese, green pepper, bacon or ham and onion and mix well.
3. Pour the egg and meat mixture in a 4-inch by 4-inch silicon baking dish (grease if you are using a normal baking dish).
4. Place the baking dish in on the 1-inch rack. Set the temperature on the 'HI' setting and bake for about 10 to 15 minutes.
5. Let the egg sit in the in the dome with the heat off for another minute.
6. Extract the egg from the silicon-baking dish and cut into pieces.
7. Serve hot with a side of baked English muffins or whole wheat bread.
8. Enjoy!

Tip:
You can add any type of meat to the omelet, just chop it into bite-sized pieces and drain all the grease from it.

NuWave Style Cheesy English Muffin Sandwich

Serves: 1

Ingredients:
- 1 large egg
- 1 slice Canadian bacon
- 1 English muffin, split in half
- 1 slice American cheese
- Salt, to taste
- Pepper, to taste

Directions:
1. Spray a large custard cup with cooking spray or grease it with some butter.
2. Crack the egg into the custard cup and slowly break the yolk using a fork. Do not beat the egg.
3. Season the egg with salt and pepper to taste. (You can add more seasoning if you want.)
4. In the liner pan, place the English muffin halves. Place the egg on a 3-inch rack.
5. Set the temperature setting to 'HI' and bake for about 5 to 7 minutes.
6. When the time is up, place the Canadian bacon the rack, right next to the egg.
7. Place the cheese slice on the muffin and continue baking for 2 more minutes.
8. Once done, extract the egg from the custard bowl and place on the cheese covered English muffin half. Place the Canadian bacon on the egg and cover with the leftover English muffin halve.
9. Serve immediately with condiments of your choice (if you want) or with some fresh fruit juice.
10. Enjoy!

Tip:
1. If you want a cheesier breakfast, place an American cheese slice on both halves of the English muffin.
2. The Canadian bacon can be substituted with frozen breakfast sausage patties.

Crunchy Low Calorie French Toast

Serves: 3

Ingredients:
- 1/4 loaf bread (any type), chopped into thick sliced
- 1/2 cup corn flakes, crumbed
- 1/2 (16-ounce) container egg substitute

Directions:
1. Pour the egg substitute in a shallow pan.
2. Place the bread slices in the egg substitute and soak for a minute or two.
3. Place the crumbled cornflakes in a flat dish and coat the egg substitute soaked bread slices with the crumbled cornflakes.
4. Place the bread slices on the 3-inch rack and bake on the 'HI' setting for about 12 to 15 minutes.
5. Allow to cool a bit before serving with a side of fresh fruit or a dollop of whipped cream if you wish.

Steak, Eggs & Cheese Stuffed Tomatoes

Serves: 2

Ingredients:
- 2 (4-ounce) sirloin steak
- 1 tomato, cut into halves and seeds removed
- Seasoned salt to taste
- 4 tablespoons Parmesan cheese, grated
- 4 large eggs
- 2 tablespoon butter
- 2 scallions, thinly sliced

Directions:
1. Crack open the eggs in a shallow dish that is ovenproof.
2. Break the yolks carefully and place the dish on the liner pan.
3. Carefully slice the rounded side of the tomato halves a little so that they can stand on their bottom.
4. Stuff the tomato halves with the grated cheese.
5. Add the seasoned salt to the steaks and rub it in using your fingers.
6. Place the cheese stuffed tomato halves and the steak on the 3-inch rack.
7. Set you NuWave oven to the 'HI' setting and bake for about 9 to 10 minutes from a medium steak.
8. Cut the egg into two halves.
9. On two serving plates, place the steaks, cheese stuffed tomato halves and the eggs.
10. Serve immediately with some toasted bread.
11. Enjoy!

Delicious Ham and Cheese Strata

Serves: 3 - 4

Ingredients:
- 5 bread slices
- 3 ounces Swiss cheese, shredded
- 3/4 cups ham, cubed
- 3 ounces Cheddar cheese, shredded
- 1/4 teaspoon salt
- 2 eggs
- 1/2 teaspoon onion powder
- 3/4 cups milk
- 1/2 teaspoon dry mustard
- 3/4 cups corn flakes
- ¼ teaspoon red chili powder
- 2 tablespoons butter, melted

Directions:
1. Remove the crust from the bread slices and place in the bottom of a 10-inch baking pan or a 4-inch by 4-inch silicon baking pan.
2. Put a layer of ham on top of the bread, topped by a layer of Swiss cheese, followed by a layer of Cheddar cheese. Repeat until all the ham and cheese is over.
3. Combine the milk, salt, onion powder, dry mustard, red chili powder and eggs together. Whisk until frothy.
4. Pour the prepared egg mixture over the layers of ham and cheese.
5. Let it stand for a few minutes until the bread absorbs the liquid.
6. Combine the melted butter and cornflakes in a small mixing bowl and pour over cheese layers.
7. Place the baking pan on the 1-inch rack and bake on the 'HI' setting for about 20 to 25 minutes until you see a crust forming.
8. When the top of the strata starts browning, cover the baking pan with a sheet of heavy-duty aluminum foil loosely and bake for another 10 to 15 minutes.
9. When the timer rings, leave the baking pan in for another 1 or 2 minutes.
10. Remove the baking pan from the oven and cool for a few minutes before slicing the strata (do not slice in the silicon pan as the knife can damage the silicon).
11. Serve hot with some fresh fruit juice.
12. Enjoy!

Ham & Eggs Scramble

Serves: 2

Ingredients:
- 4 large eggs
- Salt, to taste
- 4 tablespoons parsley, chopped
- 6 ounces ham, chopped
- 4 ounces Cheddar cheese, shredded
- Pepper, to taste

Directions:
1. Place the eggs in a medium sized mixing bowl and whisk well using a wire whisk until fluffy.
2. Add in the parsley and mix well.
3. Top with the Cheddar cheese and ham and mix well until well combined.
4. Season to taste.
5. Pour the egg mix into a shallow ovenproof baking dish.
6. Place the baking dish on a 3-inch rack and bake on the 'HI' setting for about 8 to 10 minutes.
7. Mix using a spatula and continue cooking for about 2 to 3 minutes.
8. Serve hot with a side of toasted bagel
9. Enjoy!

Deliciously Cheesy Asparagus Frittatas

Serves: 5 – 6

Ingredients:
- 1/2 teaspoon butter
- 1/2 teaspoon chives, coarsely chopped
- 1 cup grated white Cheddar, divided into ¼, ¼ & ½
- 10 spears fresh asparagus, trimmed
- 1 small yellow onion, peeled and chopped
- 6 eggs, lightly beaten
- 1 small carrot, peeled, trimmed and finely grated
- 1/2 cup milk
- 1/2 cup self-rising flour
- 1/2 teaspoon salt
- ¼ teaspoon freshly ground black pepper

Directions:
1. Grease a 6-cup Bundt pan with some butter and keep aside.
2. Combine about 1/4 cup of the grated white Cheddar and ¼ teaspoon chives together in a small bowl and keep aside.
3. Salt a large pot of water generously and heat over a high flame until bubbling. Lower the heat to a medium low and add in the asparagus spears.
4. Continue heating on a high flame for about 4 to 5 minutes or until the asparagus spears are tender.
5. Drain the asparagus spears from the water and place under cold running water for a few minutes until cool enough to handle.
6. Pat dry the asparagus spears using a kitchen towel, until dry.
7. Chop the asparagus spears into ¼th-inch pieces and place the asparagus pieces in a large bowl.
8. Add in the remaining 1/4-cup of grated white Cheddar cheese, onions, flour, salt, eggs, carrots, milk and pepper to the bowl containing the asparagus and mix well.
9. Pour the prepared mix into the greased Bundt pan and place it on the 1-inch rack in your NuWave oven.

10. Bake on the 'HI' setting for 45 to 55 minutes or until firm.
11. Once done, allow the Bundt pan to cool until manageable and invert the frittatas onto a plate.
12. Sprinkle the remaining ½ cup grated white Cheddar cheese and the remaining ¼ teaspoon chives on the frittatas.
13. Return the frittatas to the Bundt pan and place on the 1-inch rack.
14. Bake on the 'HI' setting for another 2 to 3 minutes or until the cheese melts.
15. Serve hot.
16. Enjoy!

English Muffin and Egg Casserole

Serves: 3 – 4

Ingredients:
- 1/2 (12-ounce) package English muffins
- 3 eggs
- 3 slices (2 ounces) Canadian bacon, chopped
- 3/4 cups milk
- 1 tablespoons fresh lemon juice
- 1 tablespoons mayonnaise
- 1 teaspoons fresh lemon zest
- Butter or non-stick cooking spray (optional)

Directions:
1. Cut the English muffins into two halves and then chop into 1-inch cubes.
2. Crack the eggs in a large mixing bowl and pour in the milk. Whisk until fluffy.
3. Add in the chopped Canadian bacon, mayonnaise, fresh lemon juice and fresh lemon zest to it and mix well until combined.
4. Add the English muffin cubes in to the egg mixture and mix until well coated.
5. Spray a 4-inch by 4-inch baking dish with cooking spray or grease it with butter.
6. Pour the prepared egg mixture into the prepped baking dish and cover with a sheet of aluminum foil. Refrigerate for 6 to 8 hours or overnight.
7. Remove the aluminum foil and set it aside.
8. Place the uncovered baking dish on the 1inch rack.
9. Bake on the 'HI' setting for about 45 to 50 minutes.
10. Cover using the reserved aluminum foil and continue baking for another 15 to 20 minutes.
11. Serve hot with some freshly squeezed orange juice on the side.
12. Enjoy!

Potato and Pork Breakfast Bake

Serves: 12

Ingredients:
- 1 1/2 pound new potatoes, scrubbed well, diced
- 1 1/2 cup green or red peppers, diced
- 1/2 cup leeks, sliced
- 2 teaspoon garlic, minced
- 2 tablespoon dark chili powder
- 4 tablespoons olive oil
- 2 cup spicy pork sausage, diced
- 4 eggs
- 1 cup pepper jack cheese
- Kosher salt, to taste
- Freshly ground black pepper, to taste

Directions:
1. Combine the potatoes, peppers, olive oil, freshly ground black pepper, leeks, garlic, chili powder and salt together in a large mixing bowl.
2. Place the mixture into a deep 10-inch baking pan.
3. Place the pan on the 3-inch rack and bake for about 10 to 15 minutes on the 'HI' setting.
4. Carefully remove the pan from the oven and add in the diced spicy pork sausage. Mix well.
5. Return the pan into the oven and continue cooking on the 'HI' setting for another 7 to 8 minutes.
6. Top with the pepper jack cheese and bake for another 3 to 5 minutes on the 'HI' setting or until the cheese melts.
7. Crack the eggs directly on the melted cheese, taking care that you do not break the yolk.
8. Lower the heat setting to the '9' level and bake for another 5 minutes or until the eggs are just set.
9. Serve hot.
10. Enjoy!

Brunch Bread Pudding

Serves: 2 – 3

Ingredients:
- 1 tablespoons olive oil
- 2 mushrooms, sliced
- 1/4 cup leeks, sliced
- 1 green onions, sliced
- 2 eggs
- 1 cups turkey breakfast sausage, large diced
- 1/2 cup heavy cream
- 1/2 cup Gouda cheese, shredded
- 1/2 cup milk
- 2 cups Hawaiian bread, diced into 1-inch cubes
- Kosher salt, to taste
- Freshly ground black pepper, to taste

Directions:
1. Combine the olive oil, mushrooms, sausage, leeks and onions together in a 10-inch ovenproof baking dish.
2. Season to taste with the kosher salt and freshly ground black pepper.
3. Place the baking dish on the 3-inch rack and cook on the '8' setting of your NuWave oven for about 10 minutes, pausing around the 5 minute mark to give it a stir.
4. While the mushroom and sausage mixture cooks, crack the eggs open in a large mixing bowl. Add in the Gouda, heavy cream and milk and whisk with a wire whisk until well combined. Keep aside.
5. Once the mushroom and sausage mix is cooked, place the cubes of bread in a separate bowl.
6. Pour the egg and milk mixture onto the bread cubes and mix well until well incorporated.
7. Pour the bread and egg mixture onto the cooked sausage and mushroom mixture. Mix well until well combined.

8. Place the baking pan on a 1-inch rack and bake on the '8' setting of your NuWave oven for 45 to 50 minutes or until set.
9. If the top starts browning too fast, cover the pan with a sheet of heavy-duty aluminum foil to ensure that the top does not burn while the insides cook.
10. Serve hot, topped with some fresh herbs or your favorite salsa.
11. Enjoy!

Delicious Blueberry and Pecan Streusel Cake

Serves: 8

Ingredients for the cake:
- 1 cup fresh or frozen blueberries
- 2 cups and 3 tablespoons all-purpose flour
- 2 teaspoons baking powder
- ¾ cup sugar
- ¼ teaspoon salt
- ½ cup milk
- 1 egg
- ½ cup butter, softened
- 1 cup chopped pecans

Ingredients for the Streusel Topping:
- ⅓ cup all-purpose flour
- ¼ cup cold butter
- ½ cup sugar

Directions:
1. For the Streusel topping, combine the all-purpose flour and sugar together in a small mixing bowl.
2. Add in the butter and keep cutting in, until the mixture gets a crumbly – flakey texture.
3. Combine the all-purpose flour, baking powder, sugar and salt together in a large mixing bowl.
4. In a small mixing bowl combine the butter, milk and eggs together and whisk well until well combined.
5. Pour the wet ingredients into the dry ingredients and fold until it forms a smooth batter.
6. Lightly dust the blueberries and pecans in some icing sugar and add to the batter. Mix well until incorporated.
7. Grease a 9-inch spring form pan with some butter and dust with some flour.

8. Pour the prepared cake batter into the greased and dusted pan.
9. Top the cake batter with the prepared Streusel topping mix.
10. Place the extender ring on the base tray of your NuWave oven.
11. Place the spring form pan on the 1-inch rack and bake on the '8' setting for about 35 to 45 minutes or until a skewer poked into the center of the cake comes out clean.
12. Remove the pan from the oven and cool in the pan for 5 minutes.
13. Remove the cake from the oven and cool on a wire rack for another 10 minutes.
14. Slice and serve warm topped with some vanilla ice cream or a dollop of whipping cream.
15. Enjoy!

Mini Crustless Quiche

Makes 48 mini quiches or 24 regular quiches

Ingredients:
- 6 large eggs
- 1/2 cup whole milk
- 6 large egg yolks
- 1/2 cup heavy cream
- 1/2 teaspoon ground black pepper
- 1 teaspoon kosher salt
- 1 pound mixed bell peppers, seeded and diced

Directions:
1. Crack the eggs into a large mixing bowl. Add in the egg yolks, cream, pepper, milk and salt to the bowl. Whisk well using a wire whisk until well combined and lightly fluffy.
2. Pour the egg mixture into a large glass jar or pitcher (or a cake batter dispenser if you have one!) and keep aside.
3. Place about 24 silicon mini cupcake liners (or 12 regular liners) on the rack. Spray them with cooking spray or lightly grease them.
4. Take about half the peppers and divide them equally between the cupcake liners. Pour the egg mixture on the peppers until the fill line.
5. Bake the quiches for about 20 to 25 minutes on the 'HI' setting or until set.
6. Cool the quiches in the liners for a few minutes before unmolding.
7. Repeat the process again with the remaining batter until all the quiches are done.
8. Serve hot.
9. Enjoy!

Appetizers

Delicious Cereal Party Mix

Makes: 3 cups

Ingredients:
- 1 cup bite size corn square cereal
- 1/2 cup pretzel knots
- 1 cup bite size rice square cereal
- 1/8 cup packed brown sugar
- 1/4 cup sliced almonds
- 3/4 tablespoon butter
- 1/8 teaspoon baking soda
- 3/4 tablespoon light-colored corn syrup
- 1/4 cup dried cranberries

Directions:
1. Place the bite size corn cereal, bite size rice cereal, almond and pretzels together in a large bowl. Mix well and keep aside.
2. Place the brown sugar, corn syrup and butter together in a large saucepan.
3. Heat on a medium high flame and keep mixing until the mixtures starts bubbling lightly.
4. Stop stirring and let the mixture simmer for another 3 to 4 minutes.
5. Take the saucepan off heat and add in the baking soda. Mix well.
6. Pour the prepared sugar mixture over the prepared cereal mix and toss well until well coated.
7. Pour the prepared cereal and sugar mix on the liner pan in a single layer.
8. Bake on the 'HI' setting for about 9 to 10 minutes.
9. Remove the pan from the oven and stir well using a wooden spoon.
10. Pop the liner pan back into the NuWave oven and bake for another 5 to 7 minutes.
11. Lightly grease a sheet of aluminum foil with some butter or spray with cooking spray and empty the hot party mix onto it.
12. Once cooled, break the party mix into pieces and add in the dried fruit.
13. Mix well and serve immediately.
14. Store in an airtight container, away from direct sunlight.
15. Enjoy!

Sour Cream and Ranch Stuff Potato Bites

Serves: 4

Ingredients:
- 4 medium baked potatoes
- 2 packets ranch seasoning
- 1/2 cup low fat sour cream
- 2 cups Cheddar cheese, shredded
- Bacon pieces, cooked (optional)
- Green onions (optional)

Directions:
1. Place the potatoes on the 1-inch rack and lightly fork. Bake them on the 'HI' setting for about 45 to 50 minutes.
2. Remove the potatoes from the oven and cool for about 5 to 10 minutes.
3. Cut the potatoes in halves, lengthwise and use a spoon to scoop out the filling from the skin.
4. Place the potato in a mixing bowl. Add in the seasoning mix and the low fat sour cream to it. Mix well until well combined.
5. Spoon the prepared mixture into the skins and top with some cheese.
6. Place the prepared skins on a 3-inch rack and bake on the 'HI' setting for about 7 to 10 minutes or until the cheese is bubbly.
7. Top with bacon and green onions and serve immediately.
8. Enjoy!

Bacon Wrapped Shrimp Bites

Serves: 3

Ingredients:
- 6 jumbo shrimp, cut in half or 12 small shrimp
- 3 slices bacon
- 1/8 cup sliced water chestnuts

Directions:
1. Chop the bacon into 4 equal parts.
2. Place a chestnut slice on a shrimp.
3. Roll the bacon carefully over the shrimp and chestnut and secure it in place using a toothpick.
4. Place the prepared shrimp rolls on the 3-inch rack and bake on the 'HI' setting for about 8 to 10 minutes per side.
5. Serve hot with a side of your favorite condiment and a fresh salad.
6. Enjoy!

Tip:
You can also use tofu, mussels or chicken livers in place of the shrimp.

Toasted Bacon, Apple and Grilled Cheese Sandwiches

Serves: 4

Ingredients:
- 4 tablespoons butter, softened
- 8 slices sourdough bread
- 12 ounces smoked Gouda cheese, sliced
- 12 strips apple wood smoked bacon, cooked
- 2 honey crisp apples, cored and sliced
- Salt to taste

Directions:
1. Apply about ½ tablespoon of butter on one side of the sourdough bread slice.
2. With the buttered slice up, place four slices of the buttered bread on a 3-inch rack.
3. Toast the bread on the 'HI' setting for about 3 to 4 minutes.
4. Flip the bread over and place about 3 strips of bacon and 1 slice of cheese on each slice of the bread.
5. Place the apple slices in a single layer over the cheese.
6. Place the remaining buttered slices over the apple slices with their buttered side up.
7. Toast the sandwiches for another 4 to 5 minutes on the 'HI' setting.
8. Once toasted, remove the toasted sandwiches on a cutting board and slice diagonally before serving.
9. Serve warm.
10. Enjoy!

Goat Cheese, Pear and Walnut Crostini

Serves: 3 – 4

Ingredients:
- 1/4 cup coarsely chopped walnuts
- 1/2 tablespoon brown sugar
- 1/2 tablespoon plus 1 teaspoon honey
- 1 large Bosc pear, peeled, cored and cut lengthwise into wedges about ½-inch thick
- 1 (6-inch) baguette
- 1/2 tablespoon olive oil
- 3 ounces goat cheese
- Extra-virgin olive oil
- 1/2 cup arugula or basil (optional)
- Coarse sea salt or kosher salt

Directions:
1. Place the walnuts in a small mixing bowl. Add in the 1-teaspoon honey and the brown sugar. Toss well until the walnuts are well coated.
2. Place the walnuts in a single layer in the liner pan. Place the 3-inch rack over the walnut filled liner pan.
3. Slice the baguette into ½-inch thick slices and arrange on the 3-inch rack in a single layer.
4. Lightly brush olive oil over the baguette slices.
5. Set your NuWave oven on the 'HI' setting and toast the bread and walnuts for about 4 to 5 minutes.
6. Remove the bread covered 3-inch rack from the oven and toast the walnuts for an additional 4 to 6 minutes.
7. Place the toasted bread slices on a flat surface and arrange the pear wedges on the bread in a single layer.
8. Spread the goat cheese on the pears.
9. Top the cheese with the toasted walnuts and garnish with some basil or arugula.
10. Lightly pour some olive oil and honey over the crostini and season to taste with a pinch of kosher salt or sea salt.
11. Rest the crostini for about 30 minutes before serving. This helps in enhancing the cheesy flavor in the crostini.
12. Serve with a side of toasted walnuts.
13. Enjoy!

Cheesy Mixed Vegetable Quesadillas

Serves: 4

Ingredients:
- 1/2 small zucchini, grated and drained
- 1/2 small red onion, chopped
- 1/2 cup frozen corn, defrosted and drained
- 1 jalapeño pepper, seeded and chopped
- 1/4 teaspoon salt
- 1/2 (15-ounce) can black beans, drained and rinsed
- 1/8 teaspoon freshly ground black pepper
- 1/2 pound Monterey-Jack cheese, grated
- 1/2 teaspoon chili powder
- 4 (8-inch) flour tortillas
- 1 tablespoon vegetable oil

Directions:
1. Place the zucchini, onion, beans, pepper, corn, jalapeños, salt and chili powder together in a large mixing bowl. Toss well until well seasoned.
2. Place the tortillas in a single layer on a 3-inch rack.
3. Divide the vegetable mixture into 4 parts and place each part on a tortilla. Sprinkle each tortilla with a good amount of cheese.
4. Bake the tortillas on the 'HI' setting for about 5 to 7 minutes or until the cheese has melted.
5. Remove tortillas from the oven and fold into half.
6. Slice the quesadillas into halves and serve with your favorite salsa or with a condiment of your choice.
7. Enjoy!

Loaded NuWave Nachos

Serves: 2

Ingredients:
- 1/2 bag tortilla chips
- 1/2 package taco seasoning
- 1/2 pound cooked ground beef
- 2 tomatoes, diced
- 1/2 jar pickled jalapeños
- 1/2 can sliced olives
- 1/2 jar salsa
- 1/2 bag shredded Cheddar cheese
- 1/4 cup sour cream

Directions:
1. Pour the tortilla chips into the liner pan and arrange in an even layer.
2. Place the ground beef in a mixing bowl and sprinkle the taco seasoning over it. Mix well until combined.
3. Spread the ground beef over the tacos in an even layer.
4. Top the beef with the tomatoes, salsa, jalapeños and sour cream.
5. Pour the cheese generously over the veggies and bake on the 'HI' setting for about 10 to 15 minutes or until the cheese is bubbling.
6. Remove the nachos from the oven and cool.
7. Serve immediately.
8. Enjoy!

Delicious 3 Cheese Garlic Bread

Serves: 2

Ingredients:
- 1/2 loaf Italian bread, sliced in half
- 1 cloves minced garlic
- 3 tablespoons olive oil
- 1/4 teaspoon dried oregano
- 1/2 cup shredded Asiago cheese
- 1 tablespoons grated Parmesan cheese
- 1/2 cup mozzarella cheese

Directions:
1. Combine the garlic, olive oil and oregano together in a small mixing bowl.
2. Using a pastry brush, brush the prepared mix onto the cut sides of the bread.
3. In a medium sized mixing bowl, place the Asiago cheese and top with the Parmesan cheese. Add in the mozzarella cheese and mix well until combined.
4. Place the garlic and olive oil brushed bread with its cut side up on the 1-inch rack.
5. Top the bread with a copious amount of cheese and bake on the 'HI' setting for about 12 to 15 minutes or until the cheese has completely melted.
6. Cool the bread a little, and once slightly firm, slice the bread into ½-inch slices.
7. Serve immediately, topped with some chili flakes and pizza seasoning.
8. Enjoy!

Delicious Cheddar, Jalapeño & Corn Muffins

Makes: 6 muffins

Ingredients:
- 1/2 cup Cheddar cheese, shredded
- 3/4 cups flour
- 1/2 cup sugar
- 3/4 cups cornmeal
- 1/2 teaspoon baking powder
- 1/2 teaspoon salt
- 1/4 teaspoon baking soda
- 5 tablespoons milk
- 5 tablespoons sour cream
- 1/2 stick butter
- 1/2 jalapeño, chopped and seeded
- 1 egg
- 1/2 onion, diced and caramelized

Directions:
1. Combine the flour, sugar, cornmeal, baking powder, salt and baking soda together in a medium sized mixing bowl.
2. In another bowl, combine Cheddar cheese, milk, sour cream, butter jalapeños, egg and onion together.
3. Pour the wet ingredients onto the dry ingredients and fold well until well combined. Do not over mix or the batter will fall flat.
4. Spray 6 muffin cups with cooking spray or grease them using a little melted butter.
5. Pour the batter into the 6 prepared muffin cups.
6. Place the batter filed cups on the 3-inch rack and bake on the 'HI' setting for about 20 to 25 minutes.
7. Remove the muffin cups from the oven and cool for about 5 minutes.
8. Remove the muffins from the muffin cups and cool on a wire rack for about 10 to 15 minutes.
9. Serve warm with a side of your favorite salsa or condiment.
10. Enjoy!

Cheesy Garlic Buttermilk Biscuit Bread Bites

Makes: 6 bread bites

Ingredients:
- 1/2 (16-ounce) tube refrigerated buttermilk biscuits
- 1 tablespoon freshly grated Parmesan
- 2 tablespoons unsalted butter, melted
- 2 cloves garlic, minced
- 1/4 teaspoon dried basil
- 1/4 teaspoon dried oregano
- 1/4 teaspoon dried parsley flakes
- Pinch of salt

Directions:
1. Arrange 6 silicon cupcake liners on the 1-inch rack.
2. Place the refrigerated buttermilk biscuit dough on a flat and floured work surface
3. Using an extremely sharp knife cut every piece of the buttermilk biscuit dough into 8 even slices. Keep aside.
4. Place the butter, garlic, basil, salt, Parmesan, oregano and parsley together in a large mixing bowl. Whisk together using a wire whisk until its gets a smooth texture.
5. Pour about 1 tablespoon of the prepared herb butter mixture into a small bowl and keep aside.
6. Place the biscuit pieces into the herbed butter mix and toss until well coated.
7. Take about 5 to 7 slices of the herbed butter covered dough and press them together in the bottom of each greased cupcake liner.
8. Add the extender ring to the base tray of your NuWave oven.
9. Close the dome of your NuWave oven and bake on the '8' setting of your NuWave oven for about 18 to 20 minutes.
10. Using a pastry brush, lightly brush the reserved herbed butter mix onto the bread bites and serve immediately.
11. Enjoy!

Tips:
1. If you do not wish to bake individual muffin cups, bake the bread bites in a loaf pan or a divided silicon baking pan on the 1-inch rack on the '8' setting for 28 to 30 minutes.
2. You can use any other cheese, such as mozzarella or Cheddar or even Gouda cheese instead of Parmesan cheese.

Baked Herb Cheese Fries

Makes: 1 pound

Ingredients:
- 1/2 pound 3-cheese blend, shredded
- 1/2 tablespoon fresh thyme, chopped
- 1/2 tablespoon fresh oregano, chopped
- 1/2 tablespoon fresh rosemary, chopped
- ¼ teaspoon freshly ground black pepper
- 1 pound frozen fries
- Pinch of kosher salt
- 1 tablespoon olive oil

Directions:
1. Place the fresh thyme, fresh rosemary, fresh oregano, freshly ground black pepper and kosher salt together in a small mixing bowl. Mix well until well combined.
2. Place the frozen fries in a large mixing bowl and pour the olive oil over the frozen fries. Toss well until the fries are well coated with olive oil.
3. Pour the seasoning mix over the olive oil coated fries and toss well until the fries are well coated with the seasoning.
4. Place the seasoning coated fries on the 3-inch rack in an even layer.
5. Set your NuWave oven on the 'HI' setting and bake for about 8 to 10 minutes.
6. Once the fries get a crispy exterior, open the dome of your NuWave oven and transfer the fries from the 3-inch rack to the liner pan.
7. Top the fries with the shredded 3 cheese blend and bake for another 5 to 7 minutes on the 'HI' setting or until the cheese has melted.
8. Once the fries are done, promptly open the dome of the oven so that all the excess moisture is released and the fries remain crispy.
9. Serve hot.
10. Enjoy!

Tips:
1. If you do not have fresh spices, you can use the dried ones too. Just halve the quantity of spices.
2. When the fries are baking initially, make sure you pause the oven at regular intervals to toss the fries. This ensures that all the fries are evenly browned.
3. If you are using fresh potatoes instead of the frozen fries, add about 5 minutes to the total cooking time.

Italian Bread Loaf Pizza

Serves: 2

Ingredients:
- 2 (12-inch) loaves Italian bread
- 4 tablespoons olive oil
- 2 tablespoon garlic, chopped
- 1 cup marinara sauce
- 2/3 cup Parmesan cheese, shredded
- 6 baby Portabella mushrooms, sliced
- 2/3 cup red onions, sliced
- 2/3 cup green pepper, sliced
- 1/2 cup tomato, diced
- 1 cup mozzarella cheese, shredded
- 2 tablespoons basil, sliced

Directions:
1. Slice the loaves of bread in half lengthwise. Use a serrated knife dipped into hot water (and wiped before cutting) for best results.
2. Combine the olive oil and chopped garlic together in a small bowl and set aside for about 5 to 10 minutes so that the olive oil gets infused with the garlic.
3. Using a pastry brush spread the prepared garlic olive oil on the bread.
4. Using a spoon spread the marinara sauce in a thin layer over the bread. Top the marinara sauce layer with an even layer of Parmesan cheese.
5. Add the mushrooms, peppers, onions and tomatoes over the Parmesan cheese and top the vegetables with a layer of mozzarella cheese.
6. Place the prepared bread loaf halves on a 1-inch rack and bake on the 'HI' setting for about 10 minutes or until the cheese melts.
7. Garnish the pizza with some basil.
8. Slice your pizza and serve immediately.
9. Enjoy!

Cheese Burst Bacon Wrapped Tater Tots

Serves: 2

Ingredients:
- 1 cup frozen tater tots, brought down to room temperature
- 1/2 ounce sharp Cheddar cheese, cut into ¼-inch squares
- 2 slices bacon, cut into quarters
- 2 tablespoons brown sugar
- 1/2 tablespoon chopped parsley (optional)

Directions:
1. Wrap a piece of bacon around a tater tot and cheese square.
2. Place the brown sugar in a flat plate and lightly roll the bacon wrapped tater tots in the brown sugar. Lightly press while rolling to ensure that the brown sugar sticks to the surface of the bacon.
3. Place the bacon wrapped and brown sugar covered tater tots on the liner pan, with their seam side facing down.
4. Bake on the 'HI' setting for about 25 to 30 minutes. Make sure you flip the tater tots over around the halfway mark.
5. Serve immediately, topped with some parsley.
6. Enjoy!

Delicious Chicken in Alfredo Sauce Roll Ups

Serves: 4

Ingredients for the Rolls:
- 1/2 tablespoon olive oil
- 1/2 (8-ounce) package cream cheese, room temperature
- 1/2 skinless and boneless chicken breast
- 2 tablespoons freshly grated Parmesan cheese
- 1/4 teaspoon garlic powder
- 1 tablespoon chopped chives
- Kosher salt, to taste
- 1/2 (8-ounce) tube crescent rolls
- Freshly ground black pepper to taste
- 1/4 cup Italian style breadcrumbs

Ingredients for the Sauce:
- 1/2 tablespoon unsalted butter
- 1/4 cup milk
- 1/2 tablespoon all-purpose flour
- Kosher salt, to taste
- 1/4 cup Parmesan cheese or to taste
- Freshly ground black pepper, to taste

Directions for the Rolls:
1. Season the chicken breast with some salt and pepper.
2. Place the seasoned chicken breast on the 3-inch rack.
3. Bake the chicken breast on the 'HI' setting for 12 to 15 minutes per side.
4. Remove the chicken breast from the rack and cool to room temperature. Once cooled, shred the chicken using two forks.
5. Place the shredded chicken, Parmesan cheese, garlic powder, pepper, cream cheese, chives and pepper together in a large mixing bowl. Mix well until well combined.
6. Remove the crescent rolls from the tube and cut into 4 triangles.

7. Place about a tablespoon of the prepared chicken mix onto the triangle and roll up the triangle, starting from the wide end and tuck in the edges beneath the filling.
8. Place the breadcrumbs in a flat plate and roll each triangle in the breadcrumbs. Press lightly so that the breadcrumbs stick to the rolls.
9. Place the breadcrumb-coated rolls in the liner pan with the seam side down.
10. Bake on the 'HI' setting for about 12 to 15 minutes or until the rolls turn golden brown.

Directions for the Sauce:
1. Place butter in a large 1-quart saucepan and heat over a medium low flame until the butter melts.
2. Add the flour to the melted butter and whisk using a wire whisk, until the flour turns light brown.
3. Slowly, add the milk into the flour and cook for about 5 to 7 minutes, whisking vigorously and continuously until the sauce slightly thickens.
4. Season to taste with salt and pepper.
5. Add in the cheese, about ½ cup at a time and mix well until smooth.
6. Place the rolls in a serving plate and top with the hot sauce.
7. Serve immediately.
8. Enjoy!

Poultry Recipes

Crispy Ginger and Honey Crusted Chicken

Serves: 2

Ingredients:
- 2 (4-ounce) skinless and boneless chicken breasts
- 1/2 tablespoon orange juice
- 1/2 tablespoon honey
- 1/4 teaspoon ground ginger
- Dash red pepper flakes (optional)
- 1/8 teaspoon black pepper
- 1/4 teaspoon dried parsley flakes
- 1/2 cup crushed corn flakes

Directions:
1. Grease a shallow 10-inch baking dish with some melted butter or spray some cooking spray in it to grease it.
2. Combine honey, ginger, red pepper flakes, orange juice and black pepper together in a small mixing bowl. Whisk well until well combined.
3. Use a pastry brush and brush the prepared marinade over the chicken breasts.
4. Mix together the parsley and corn flakes together and roll the marinated chicken breasts in it.
5. Place the corn flake covered chicken breasts in the prepared baking dish and place the baking dish on the 3-inch rack.
6. Bake the chicken breasts on the 'HI' setting for about 15 minutes on each side.
7. Once the juices run clear, the chicken is done.
8. Let it rest for a few minutes before slicing it.
9. Serve with a side of roasted vegetables and mashed potatoes.
10. Enjoy!

Tips:
1. If you are using frozen chicken breasts, increase the cooking time to about 17 to 20 minutes per side.
2. If your chicken breast is smaller, it will cook faster, while a thicker chicken breast will take longer to cook.

Delicious Whole Italian Style Chicken

Serves: 4 – 6

Ingredients:
- 4 large cloves garlic, minced
- 8 tablespoons olive oil, divided
- 1 teaspoon cracked black pepper salt
- 1 teaspoon kosher salt
- 1 (3-pound) whole chicken
- 2 tablespoons chopped thyme
- 2 tablespoons chopped rosemary
- 2 tablespoons chopped oregano

Directions:
1. Combine about 2 tablespoons of olive oil, pepper and salt together in a small mixing bowl. Pour it over the chicken and rub it in using your fingers.
2. Run a thin spatula handle or a chopstick between the flesh and the flesh of the chicken.
3. Combine the remaining olive oil, rosemary, thyme, garlic and oregano together in a small mixing bowl.
4. Lightly pour this herbed oil between the flesh of the chicken and the skin of the chicken. Rub the herbed oil lightly so that it reaches all the parts of the chicken.
5. Place the chicken on the 1-inch rack breast down. Bake the chicken on the 'HI' setting for about 30 to 45 minutes.
6. Flip the chicken over and spoon the juices from the liner pan over the chicken in order to baste it.
7. Continue baking the chicken on the 'HI' setting for an additional 30 to 45 minutes.
8. Once done, let the chicken rest for a few minutes before carving it.
9. Serve hot with a side of grilled vegetables of your choice.
10. Enjoy!

Sweet & Spicy Barbeque Chicken

Serves 2

Ingredients:
- 1/2 teaspoon hot sauce
- 1/4 cup light brown sugar
- 3 tablespoons cider vinegar
- 2 tablespoons molasses
- 2 garlic cloves, minced
- 1 1/2 tablespoons Dijon mustard
- 1/4 cup ketchup
- 1/2 tablespoon vegetable oil plus extra for grates
- 1 small whole (1 1/2-pound) chicken, cut into individual pieces
- Salt, to taste
- Pepper, to taste

Directions:
1. Combine together the hot sauce, cider vinegar, brown sugar, molasses, Dijon mustard, minced garlic cloves and ketchup together in a shallow ovenproof baking dish.
2. Place this dish on a 1-inch rack and bake on the 'HI' setting for about 8 to 10 minutes.
3. Place the chicken pieces in a large mixing bowl and pour the prepared sauce over it. Toss well until all the pieces of the chicken are well coated by the sauce.
4. Place the marinated chicken pieces on a 3-inch rack with their skin sides down. Bake on the 'HI' setting for about 13 to 15 minutes.
5. Flip over the chicken and baste the chicken pieces with the extra sauce.
6. Place the chicken pieces; now skin side up, on a 3-inch rack.
7. Bake on the 'HI' setting for another 13 to 15 minutes or until a thermometer inserted in the chicken reads about 165 degrees Fahrenheit.
8. Serve hot with a side of your favorite salad.
9. Enjoy!

Spinach, Ham & Sun Dried Tomatoes Stuffed Chicken Roulade

Serves: 3

Ingredients:
- 3 (6-ounce) boneless chicken breast with skin
- Freshly ground black pepper, to taste
- Salt, to taste
- 3 slices prosciutto ham
- 12 pieces sun-dried tomatoes
- 5 ounces frozen spinach, sautéed with garlic and drained
- 1/2 teaspoon chopped garlic

Directions:
1. Take a long piece of cling wrap and cover a cutting board with it. Tuck the loose ends under the cutting board to keep the cling wrap taut.
2. Place the chicken breasts, skin side down; on the cling wrap covered board. Carefully slice the breasts open to make a butterfly cut, without completely cutting through.
3. Sprinkle a healthy amount of salt and pepper over the chicken breasts and lightly rub it with your fingers,
4. Take another long piece of the cling wrap and place it over the butterfly cut and seasoned chicken breasts.
5. Hammer on the chicken breasts using a meat tenderizer until each breast is uniformly thick.
6. Remove the cling wrap and lay a single slice of ham on each chicken breast.
7. Add about 1 ounce of spinach and about 4 pieces of sun-dried tomatoes over each ham slice.
8. Fold two long ends of the chicken breast over the filling and tightly roll the chicken breast from the shorter end.
9. Place the chicken rolls with their seam side down on a cookie sheet and refrigerate for an hour or until the roll is firm.
10. Once the chicken roll is firm, place the chicken roll on a 3-inch rack and bake for about 30 to 35 minutes on the 'HI' setting. Around the 15-minute mark, flip the roll over.
11. Remove the chicken roll from the oven and let it rest for about 5 minutes before slicing each chicken roll into 4 thick slices.
12. Serve hot with the condiments of your choice.
13. Enjoy!

Roasted Dijon and Herb Encrusted Chicken Breast

Serves: 2

Ingredients:
- 2 (5-ounce) chicken breasts, with the bone in and skin on
- 1 tablespoon Dijon mustard
- 1/2 tablespoon olive oil
- 2 sprigs parsley leaves, chopped
- 1 teaspoon garlic, chopped
- 1/2 teaspoon sugar
- 1/2 teaspoon red pepper flakes
- 1 teaspoon salt
- 1/2 teaspoon black pepper
- 1/4 yellow onion, sliced

Directions:
1. Combine together the Dijon mustard, olive oil, chopped parsley leaves, chopped garlic, sugar, red pepper flakes, salt, black pepper and sliced yellow onion together in a mixing bowl.
2. Add the chicken breasts to the prepared marinade and toss well until the chicken breasts are well coated.
3. Place the chicken breasts in an airtight container or a sealable bag and pour the leftover marinade over them.
4. Seal the container or the bag and give it a vigorous shake.
5. Refrigerate for at least 4 to 6 hours.
6. Place the marinated chicken breasts on a 3-inch rack with its skin side down.
7. Bake the chicken breasts for about 13 to 15 minutes on the 'HI' setting.
8. Flip it over and cook for another 13 to 15 minutes, and spoon some of the leftover over the chicken breasts.
9. Once cooked through, let the chicken breasts rest for about 5 minutes.
10. Serve hot over some mashed potatoes or over a bed of steamed rice.
11. Enjoy!

Chicken Parmesan

Serves: 2

Ingredients:
- 2 (5-ounce) chicken breasts
- 1/2 cup seasoned panko breadcrumbs
- 2 eggs
- 1/2 cup flour
- 1/4 tablespoon pepper
- 1/2 tablespoon kosher salt
- 1/2 (14-ounce) jar marinara sauce
- 2 slices provolone cheese

Directions:
1. Crack open the eggs in a shallow bowl and lightly season it with salt and pepper. Whisk well.
2. Place the flour in another shallow plate and season it to taste.
3. Finally, place the seasoned panko breadcrumbs in another shallow flat plate.
4. Make light indentions on the chicken breasts with a sharp knife, making sure that you don't cut through.
5. Dip the chicken breasts into the seasoned flour.
6. Then dip the flour coated chicken into the eggs.
7. Finally dip the flour and egg coated chicken into the plate with the breadcrumbs and lightly press until the breadcrumbs stick to the chicken breasts.
8. Place the breadcrumb encrusted chicken on a 3-inch rack and back on the 'HI' setting for about 15 to 17 minutes per side.
9. Place a slice of provolone on each chicken breast and continue baking on the 'HI' setting for another 2 to 3 minutes, or until the cheese melts.
10. Place the chicken breasts on serving plates and slather the marinara sauce over them.
11. Serve hot.
12. Enjoy!

Sour Cream Topped Chicken Breasts with Mushrooms & Bell Peppers

Serves: 2

Ingredients:
- Salt, to taste
- 2 (4 – 6-ounce) chicken breasts
- 1 bell pepper, cut into 1-inch pieces
- 4 large mushrooms, thinly sliced
- 1 cup sour cream
- Pepper, to taste

Directions:
1. Place the chicken breasts in an ovenproof baking dish.
2. Add in the mushroom slices and bell pepper pieces around the chicken breasts.
3. Pour the sour cream over the ingredients and spread it in an even layer on all the ingredients using the back of a spoon.
4. Season to taste with salt and pepper.
5. Place the baking dish on a 3-inch rack and cook on the 'HI' setting for about 13 to 15 minutes.
6. Flip the chicken breast over and continue cooking for another 13 to 15 minutes.
7. Place the chicken breast on a serving plate and serve hot with a side of sour cream covered mushrooms and bell peppers.
8. Enjoy!

Tip:
1. If the chicken breasts you are using are frozen, increase the cooking time to about 15 to 17 minutes per side.
2. The cooking times given in this recipe are approximate. Actual cooking times may vary according to the size and thickness of the chicken breast you are using.

Delicious Chicken Bites with a Wasabi Mayonnaise Dipping Sauce

Serves: 2

Ingredients:
- 1 ½ (1-pound) chicken breasts, boneless and skinless cut into ½-inch strips, crosswise
- 1/2 teaspoon baking soda
- 1/3 cup white flour
- 1/4 cup Parmesan cheese
- 1/4 teaspoon paprika
- 1/4 teaspoon garlic salt
- 1/4 teaspoon black pepper
- 1 1/2 tablespoons extra-virgin olive oil
- 1/2 egg, slightly beaten
- 1 teaspoon wasabi
- 1/4 cup mayonnaise

Directions:
1. Grease a 3-inch cooking rack with some melted butter or spray it with some cooking spray.
2. In a large food storage bag, about 1 gallon, add in the baking soda, garlic salt, flour, cheese and paprika.
3. Place the chicken strips in the egg until coated and then place the egg coated chicken strips in the bag with the dry flour mix.
4. Seal the bag shut and shake it up until all the chicken pieces are well coated.
5. Place the flour covered chicken strips on the greases 3-inch rack.
6. Lightly sprinkle olive oil all over the chicken pieces.
7. Bake on the 'HI' setting for about 11 to 13 minutes. Around the halfway mark, flip the chicken pieces over using tongs.
8. Once the chicken is done, rest it for about a minute before serving.
9. To prepare the dipping sauce combine the mayonnaise and wasabi together in a mixing bowl and whisk well until combined.

10. Serve the chicken pieces hot, accompanied by the wasabi mayonnaise dipping sauce.
11. Enjoy!

Tip:
1. If you wish for a spicier dipping sauce, increase the quantity of the wasabi you are using.
2. If you do not like wasabi, honey mustard makes a great accompaniment to this dish too!

Quick & Easy Barbeque Chicken

Serves: 2

Ingredients:
- 1/2 whole fryer chicken (1 thigh piece, 1 breast piece, 1 wing piece and 1 leg)
- 1 tablespoon honey mustard
- 1/2 cup BBQ sauce
- 1/2 tablespoon soy sauce
- 1 clove garlic, minced
- 1/2 tablespoon Worcestershire sauce

Directions:
1. Wash the chicken pieces under running water to clean them. On a 3-inch rack, place the chicken pieces in a single layer.
2. Combine the honey mustard, BBQ sauce, soy sauce, minced garlic and Worcestershire sauce together in a small mixing bowl. Whisk with a wire whisk until well combined.
3. Brush the prepared sauce over the chicken pieces using a pastry brush, reserving about half for the other side.
4. Set your NuWave oven on the 'HI' setting and grill the chicken for about 12 to 15 minutes per side.
5. When you flip the chicken pieces over, spoon the remaining prepared sauce over the chicken pieces to keep them moist.
6. Once done, remove the chicken from the oven and rest for about 5 minutes before serving.
7. Serve hot with a side of grilled vegetables and mashed potatoes.
8. Enjoy!

Hot & Spicy Buffalo Chicken Hoagie Roll Sandwiches

Serves: 2

Ingredients:
- 1 1/2 tablespoons butter, melted
- 2 hoagie rolls, split cup ranch dressing
- 1/4 cup buffalo style hot sauce, divided
- 1/4 teaspoon Creole seasoning
- 3/4 cups celery, diagonally sliced
- 3/4 cups carrots, matchstick cut
- 2 tablespoons onion, finely chopped
- 1/2 (4-ounce) package Blue cheese, crumbled
- 6 large deli-fried chicken strips (About ½ to ¾ pounds)

Directions:
1. In a small mixing bowl place the butter and about 1 teaspoon of the hot sauce together. Whisk using a wire whisk or a fork until just combined.
2. Use a pastry brush to brush the cut sides of the hoagie rolls with the prepared hot sauce butter.
3. In a liner pan, arrange the hoagie rolls in a single layer with their cut sides up.
4. In another medium sized mixing bowl, combine the ranch dressing, Creole seasoning and about1 to 1-½ teaspoons of hot sauce together.
5. Add in the celery, carrots and onion to the bowl of the dressing and toss well until all the veggies are well coated with the sauce.
6. Place the chicken in the bottom half of the hot sauce butter coated rolls.
7. Pour the remaining hot sauce over the rolls.
8. Spoon the carrot, celery and onion mixture evenly onto the chicken and top with cheese.
9. Cover with the remaining halves of the rolls.
10. Bake on the '8' setting of your NuWave oven for about 12 to 15 minutes.
11. Serve hot with a side of hot sauce.
12. Enjoy!

Tip:
If you are not a fan of Blue cheese you can add in some Parmesan cheese, mozzarella cheese or even some Swiss cheese for a change of flavor.

Oven Fried Chicken

Serves: 2

Ingredients:
- 1/4 cup buttermilk
- 2 cloves garlic, minced
- 1/2 tablespoon Dijon mustard
- 1/2 teaspoon hot sauce
- 1/4 cup all-purpose flour
- 1 ½ -2 pounds fresh chicken, cut into thighs, breast legs, and wings, skin removed
- 3/4 teaspoons paprika
- 1/2 teaspoon baking powder
- 1/2 teaspoon dried thyme
- ¼ teaspoon salt (optional)
- Non-stick cooking spray
- ¼ teaspoon pepper to taste

Directions:
1. Place the butter, garlic, mustard and hot sauce together in a small mixing bowl. Whisk well using a wire whisk until well blended.
2. Place the chicken pieces in a shallow glass-baking dish and pour the prepared butter mix over them. Using your hands, repeatedly turn the pieces over and over until all the pieces of chicken are well coated.
3. Cover the baking dish with a cling wrap and refrigerate for at least 3 to 8 hours.
4. In a large sized sealable plastic bag, add the flour, thyme, salt, paprika, baking powder and pepper.
5. Lightly tap the chicken pieces to remove the extra marinade and place the marinated chicken pieces, two at a time, in the plastic bag.
6. Seal the plastic bag and shake the bag to coat the chicken pieces.
7. Lightly tap the chicken pieces to remove the excess flour from the chicken pieces.

8. Place the flour coated chicken pieces on a 3-inch rack and grill on the 'HI' setting for about 15 to 17 minutes on each side.
9. Once the chicken is done, remove it from the oven and let it rest for about 5 minutes before serving.
10. Serve hot with the condiment of your choice.
11. Enjoy!

Tip:

If you do not have buttermilk available on hand, use milk with a teaspoon of vinegar added to it for every quart.

Grilled Cornish Game Hens with Artichokes & Potatoes

Serves: 2

Ingredients:
- 1 tablespoon lemon juice
- 1 tablespoon extra-virgin olive oil
- 2 cloves garlic
- 1/2 teaspoon oregano
- 1/4 teaspoon kosher salt
- 1/2 teaspoon thyme
- 1/4 teaspoon black pepper
- 4 ounces small potatoes, cut into quarters
- 1 can artichoke hearts, drained
- 1 (1½-pound) Cornish game hen, washed and dried with paper towel

Directions:
1. Place the lemon juice, extra-virgin olive oil, thyme, black pepper, garlic, oregano and salt together in a small mixing bowl. Whisk using a wire whisk until well combined.
2. Place the drained artichoke hearts and potatoes in a large mixing bowl. Pour the prepared seasoned oil over the potatoes and artichoke hearts and toss vigorously until well coated.
3. Use a slotted spoon to drain the excess marinade off the potatoes and artichokes and set aside.
4. Brush the remaining marinade over the game hen and make sure the wing tips of the game hen are twisted under the back.
5. Place the hen on a 1-inch rack. Place the marinated potatoes and artichokes around the marinated hen.
6. Grill on the 'HI' setting for about 18 to 20 minutes per side (raise the time to about 32 to 25 minutes per side if you are using a frozen bird).
7. Once completely cooked, remove the hen from the oven and rest for about 5 minutes before serving.
8. Using a sharp knife cut the hens from the center into two halves.
9. Serve hot with the grilled potatoes and artichokes on the side.
10. Enjoy!

Grilled Garlic & Cilantro Chicken Breasts

Serves: 3

Ingredients:
- 3 (6-ounce) chicken breasts, skinless and boneless
- 1/2 small onion, peeled
- 2 cloves garlic, peeled
- 1/2 cup loosely packed fresh cilantro leaves
- 1/2 tablespoon soy sauce
- 1/2 tablespoon granulated sugar
- 2 tablespoons lemon or lime juice
- 1/2 teaspoon black pepper

Directions:
1. Cover a cutting board with a long piece of plastic wrap and tuck the loose ends under the cutting board to keep it taut.
2. Place the chicken breasts on plastic wrap covered board and cover with another sheet of plastic wrap.
3. Using a meat tenderizer flatten the chicken breast until ½ an-inch thick.
4. Place the flattened chicken breasts in a large sealable plastic bag.
5. Place the onions, garlic and cilantro in the jar of a blender. Blitz until finely chopped.
6. Slowly add in the lemon juice, soy sauce, sugar and pepper and continue blending until it forms a smooth paste.
7. Pour the prepared sauce into the bag with the chicken breasts.
8. Seal the bag and give it a good shake until all the chicken breast pieces are well coated.
9. Refrigerate for about 2 to 4 hours.
10. Lightly drain the excess marinade from the chicken pieces and place on a 3-inch rack.
11. Grill for about 13 to 15 minutes per side. Flip it over and grill for another 13 to 15 minutes.
12. Once the chicken is done, remove the chicken pieces from the oven and rest the chicken for about 5 minutes before serving.
13. Serve hot with a condiment of your choice.
14. Enjoy!

Delicious Chicken Curry

Serves: 2

Ingredients:
- 2 (4 – 6 ounce) chicken breast, cut into bite size pieces
- 1 green bell pepper, small diced
- 2 scallion, cut into ½-inch pieces
- 4 cloves garlic, minced
- 2 tablespoon curry powder or paste
- 4 tablespoons fresh ginger, grated
- 1/2 cup sour cream
- Salt, to taste
- 2 teaspoon coriander leaves, chopped
- Freshly ground black pepper, to taste

Directions:
1. Place the chicken, green pepper, ginger, salt, scallion, garlic, curry and pepper together in a small mixing bowl. Toss well until the chicken pieces are well coated.
2. Place the chicken pieces on a 3-inch rack and grill on the 'HI' setting for about 13 to 15 minutes per side.
3. Remove the chicken pieces from the oven into a small baking dish and add in the sour cream. Mix well.
4. Place the chicken pieces with the gravy in a serving bowl and serve hot topped with the chopped coriander.
5. Serve with a side of flat bread.
6. Enjoy!

Pork Recipes

Asian Style Pork Chops with a Tangy Pineapple Relish

Serves: 2

Ingredients:
- 2 (1 – 1½ --inch thick) pork chops
- ¼ teaspoon black pepper
- 1/2 teaspoon ground ginger
- 2 tablespoons soy sauce
- 2 cloves garlic, chopped
- 2 tablespoons extra virgin olive oil
- 1/2 tablespoon brown sugar
- 2 tablespoons red onion, sliced
- 1/2 cup fresh or canned pineapple
- 1 1/2 tablespoons flat leaf parsley, chopped
- Freshly ground black pepper, to taste
- Salt, to taste

Directions:
1. Place the ginger, soy sauce, garlic, black pepper, oil and brown sugar together in a large sealable freezer safe bag. Shake vigorously until well combined.
2. Place the pork chops in the bag with the marinade. Refrigerate for about 4 to 8 hours. The longer you let it marinate, the stronger the flavor it will have.
3. Place the pork chops on the 3-inch rack and cook on the 'HI' setting for about 10 to 12 minutes per side.
4. While the pork cooks in the oven, place the pineapple, parsley, pepper, salt and onion together in a medium-mixing bowl. Mix well until just combined to make the pineapple relish.
5. When the pork is cooked to your preference, remove it from the oven and let it rest for about 5 minutes before slicing it.
6. Serve hot, topped with the pineapple relish and with a salad on the side.
7. Enjoy!

Baked Ham in Cola

Serves: 12

Ingredients:
- 1/2 cup brown sugar
- 1/2 can cola
- 1 (5-pound) ham, bone in

Directions:
1. Place the ham with its fat side down on a 1-inch rack.
2. Pour about half of the cola on the ham and grill on the 'HI' setting for about 13 to 15 minutes, per pound of ham (in this case, it should take about 65to 75 minutes)
3. Pour the sugar over the ham and pat it so that it sticks to the ham. Slowly pour the remaining cola on the ham, taking care that you do not wash the sugar off the ham.
4. Continue baking for another 15 to 17 minutes.
5. Once the ham is cooked, let it rest inside the dome for another 5 to 7 minutes.
6. Slice the ham and serve with roasted veggies and mashed potatoes on the side.
7. Enjoy!

Tips:
1. If you are using frozen ham, increase the time to about 20 to 22 minutes per pound.
2. If you wish to cook a larger ham, say about 14 pounds or so, you can easily make it in your NuWave oven by using an extender ring.
3. If making a lamb without any coating is not your thing, bread the lamb with about ¾ cup of breadcrumbs, seasoned with 1-teaspoon dry mustard and ½ teaspoon freshly ground black pepper after dunking it with cola. The cooking time will remain the same.

Thai Style Grilled Pork Tenderloin

Serves: 3

Ingredients:
- 1 (12-ounce) pork tenderloin
- 1/2 tablespoon ginger root, chopped
- 2 cloves garlic, minced
- 1 tablespoon fresh cilantro, chopped
- 1 tablespoon lime or lemon juice
- 1 1/2 tablespoons hoisin sauce
- 1/2 tablespoon soy sauce
- 1 tablespoon sweet Asian chili sauce
- 1/2 tablespoon sesame oil

Directions:
1. Place the ginger root, garlic, fresh cilantro, lemon or lime juice, hoisin sauce, soy sauce, and sweet Asian chili sauce and sesame oil together in a small mixing bowl. Whisk well using a wire whisk until well combined.
2. Place the pork tenderloin in a baking dish, just big enough to hold the pork tenderloin.
3. Pour the prepared sauce over the tenderloin and turn the tenderloin around a few times to coat.
4. Cover the baking dish with a cling wrap and refrigerate for about 2 to 6 hours.
5. Lightly shake the excess marinade off the pork tenderloin and place it on the 3-inch rack. Grill on the 'HI' setting for about 13 to 15 minutes per side. (Increase the cooking time to about 20 to 25 minutes per side if you are using frozen tenderloin).
6. Once the meat is cooked to perfection, remove it from the oven and let it rest for about 5 minutes before slicing.
7. Cut the tenderloin diagonally.
8. Serve hot with a side of mashed potatoes and roasted vegetables.
9. Enjoy!

Delicious Casserole with Sausage, Rice & Vegetables

Serves: 2 – 3

Ingredients:
- 1/2 (10½-ounce) can condensed cream of celery soup, undiluted
- 1/2 tablespoon butter or margarine
- 1/2 cup water
- 3/4 cups instant rice
- 1/2 (10-ounce) package frozen peas, thawed
- 1/2 pound sausage, sliced into ½-inch pieces
- 1/2 cup Cheddar cheese, shredded
- 1/2 (10-ounce) package frozen corn, thawed

Directions:
1. Pour the cream of celery soup into a 2-quart saucepan.
2. Add in the butter and water and mix well.
3. Heat the saucepan over a high flame until the mix starts bubbling, stirring constantly to ensure there are no lumps.
4. Add in the rice and take the saucepan off heat. Cover and let the rice stand for about 7 minutes.
5. Add in the peas, sausage and corn to the saucepan and mix well.
6. Pour the mixture into an ovenproof baking dish and place the dish in the liner pan.
7. Set the oven to the 'HI' setting and bake for about 22 to 25 minutes.
8. Sprinkle the cheese and bake for another 2 to 3 minutes or until the cheese is lightly bubbling.
9. Serve hot.
10. Enjoy!

Juicy Pork Shoulder

Serves: 2 – 3

Ingredients for the Pork:
- 1 1/2 pounds pork shoulder
- 1/8 teaspoon whole allspice
- 1/4 teaspoon cumin seeds
- 1/4 teaspoon black peppercorns
- 3 large garlic cloves, coarsely chopped
- 1 tablespoon annatto
- 3/4 teaspoon kosher salt
- 3 tablespoons fresh orange juice
- 1/2 teaspoon dried oregano, crumbled
- 3 tablespoons distilled white vinegar

Ingredients for the Dry Rub:
- 2 tablespoons paprika
- 1 tablespoon granulated onion
- 1 tablespoon plus 1 tablespoon granulated garlic
- 1 tablespoon kosher salt
- 1 tablespoon cumin
- 1 tablespoon black pepper
- 1/2 tablespoon chipotle or ancho pepper
- 1/2 tablespoon cayenne pepper
- 1 tablespoon mustard powder
- 1/2 cup brown sugar

Directions:
1. Pour the orange juice and white distilled vinegar into a large re-sealable bag.
2. Add in the whole allspice, cumin seeds, black peppercorns, garlic cloves, annatto, kosher salt and dried oregano. Seal the bag and shake it up until it is well mixed.
3. Place the pork shoulder in the bag and shake it vigorously until the pork shoulder is well coated. Refrigerate for 1 or 2 hours.
4. In a small mixing bowl, combine the paprika, granulated onion, granulated garlic, kosher salt, cumin, black pepper, chipotle or ancho pepper, cayenne powder, mustard powder and brown sugar together.
5. Once the pork shoulder is well marinated, pour the marinade from the bag onto the liner pan. Cooking the pork shoulder with the extra marinade in the liner pan keeps the pork shoulder moist and juicy.
6. Place the marinated pork shoulder on the 1-inch rack and rub the spice rub mix on all sides of the pork shoulder.
7. Grill on the '9' setting of your NuWave oven for about 60 to 70 minutes.
8. Flip the roast over and lower the heat to the '5' setting and grill for another hour.
9. Once the timer is up, reduce the heat to the '4' setting and grill for one more hour.
10. Rest the pork shoulder for a few minutes before cutting it.
11. Serve hot with a side of mashed potatoes.
12. Enjoy!

Delicious Apple & Onion Stuffed Pork Roulade

Serves: 2

Ingredients:
- 1/2 teaspoon olive oil
- 1/2 cup chopped Fuji apple
- 1/2 cup chopped onion
- 1 teaspoon minced fresh garlic
- 1/2 teaspoon chopped fresh rosemary
- 1/2 tablespoon cider vinegar
- 1 (1/2 pound) pork tenderloin, trimmed
- ¼ teaspoon freshly ground black pepper
- ¼ teaspoon kosher salt, divided

Directions:
1. Place a large skillet over a medium high flame.
2. Add the olive oil to the skillet and heat until lightly smoking.
3. Once the oil is hot, add in the onion, garlic and apple to the pan. Sauté on a medium high flame for about 5 to 7 minutes, or until tender.
4. Pour in the vinegar and top with the rosemary. Cook for a minute.
5. Empty the contents of the skillet into a small bowl and keep aside.
6. Butterfly the pork tenderloin lengthwise, starting from the center of the pork. Place the pork on a flat and clean work surface.
7. Cover the flat pork with a piece of cling wrap and pound on it with a meat tenderizer until it is uniformly thick.
8. Rub salt and pepper on the flattened pork tenderloin.
9. Spread the prepared apple mixture in a single layer over the flattened pork.
10. Tuck in the long edges and roll the pork into a tight roll from the short end.
11. Place the stuffed pork roll on a 3-inch rack with its seam side facing up.
12. Grill on the 'HI' setting for about 15 to 17 minutes per side.
13. Once done to perfection (the internal temperature of the pork should be about 145 degrees Fahrenheit), remove the pork roll from the oven and let it rest for about 5 minutes before cutting it into slices.
14. Serve hot with the condiment of your choice.
15. Enjoy!

Andouille Sausage Burgers with a Spicy Mayonnaise

Serves: 2

Ingredients for the Spicy Mayonnaise:
- 1/2 cup mayonnaise
- 1/2 teaspoon Cajun or Creole seasoning blend
- 1/2 tablespoon fresh lemon juice
- ¼ teaspoon hot pepper sauce

Ingredients for the Burger:
- 3/4 pounds ground chuck
- 1/4 pound Andouille sausage, cut into ¼-inch cubes
- Garlic, to taste
- 1/2 cup pecans, chopped and toasted
- 1/4 teaspoon ground black pepper
- 1/2 teaspoon salt
- 2 large hamburger buns

Ingredients for the Caramelized Onion:
- 3/4 pounds onions, thinly sliced
- 2 garlic cloves, minced
- 1 tablespoon olive oil plus more for brushing pan
- 1/2 tablespoon golden brown sugar

Directions:
1. Place the mayonnaise and fresh lemon juice together in a small blender.
2. Whisk until well combined.
3. Add in the Creole seasoning blend or the Cajun seasoning blend and hot pepper sauce to the blender. Blitz until smooth.
4. Empty the flavored mayonnaise into a small bowl and cover with a cling wrap. Refrigerate until you are ready to use it.
5. Place the beef in a large mixing bowl. Add in the sausage, pecans, pepper, garlic and salt to it and mix well using your hands.
6. Divide the beef mixture in two and shape the beef mix into two patties. Keep aside.
7. Combine the olive oil, brown sugar, onions and garlic together. Mix well until all the ingredients are well incorporated.
8. Spread the onion mix in the bottom of liner pan in an even layer.
9. Place the prepared patties on the 3-inch rack and grill on the 'HI' setting for about 7 to 10 minutes on each side.
10. Slice the burger bun in half and spread the prepared spicy mayonnaise on the bottom bun.
11. Place the grilled patties on the spicy mayonnaise and top with the grilled onions.
12. Serve immediately with a side of crispy French fries.
13. Enjoy!

Hot and Spicy Chorizo Burgers

Serves: 2

Ingredients:
- 1/4 pound fresh chorizo, casings removed
- 1/2 teaspoon ground cumin
- 1/4 pound lean ground beef
- 1/4 teaspoon ground coriander
- 2 cloves garlic, finely chopped
- 1 tablespoon cilantro, finely chopped and divided
- Kosher salt, to taste
- 1/4 cup mayonnaise
- Freshly ground black pepper, to taste
- 3/4 tablespoons hot sauce
- 1 tablespoon olive oil
- 1/2 teaspoon fresh lime juice
- 2 slices pepper jack cheese
- Lettuce leaves, and sliced tomatoes,
- 2 hamburger buns, lightly toasted,
- 1 ripe Hass avocado, pitted, peeled and thinly sliced

Directions:
1. Place the chorizo, cumin, ½ tablespoon cilantro, salt, beef, coriander, garlic and pepper together in a medium-mixing bowl
2. Divide the mixture into two and make 2 patties that are about 3-inches wide and about 1-inch thick each.
3. Place the prepared patties on a 3-inch rack and grill on the 'HI' setting for 8 to 10 minutes on each side.
4. While the patties cook in the oven, combine the remaining cilantro with the mayonnaise, lime juice, pepper, hot sauce and salt in a small mixing bowl. Keep aside.
5. Once the patties are done and place a slice of cheese on each patty. Continue baking on the 'HI' setting for another minute or until the cheese melts.
6. Spoon the spicy mayonnaise on the bottom buns and place the lettuce, tomato slices and avocado slices on it.
7. Top with the cheese topped burger patties and cover with the top half of the burger bun.
8. Serve hot with a side of crispy French fries.
9. Enjoy!

Tip:
For the ultimate breakfast experience, top the burger patty with a single fried egg!

Sweet and Spicy Baby Back Ribs

Serves: 4 – 6

Ingredients:
- 1/2 cup paprika
- 1/4 cup granulated onion
- 1/4 cup plus 2 tablespoons granulated garlic
- 1/4 cup kosher salt
- 1/4 cup ground cumin
- 1/4 cup ground black pepper
- 2 tablespoons chipotle or ancho pepper
- 2 tablespoons cayenne pepper
- 1/4 cup mustard powder
- 2 cups brown sugar
- 6 cups water
- 2 slabs baby back ribs
- 4 tablespoons liquid smoke

Directions:
1. Combine the paprika, granulated onion, granulated garlic, kosher salt, ground cumin, ground black pepper, chipotle or ancho pepper, cayenne pepper and mustard powder together in a medium sized mixing bowl. Whisk well until all the ingredients are well incorporated.
2. Add in the brown sugar to the spice mix and mix well to combine.
3. Spoon the prepared spice rub on the slab of baby ribs and coat the baby ribs on all sides. Make sure that you rub the spice rub into all the boney and fatty areas of the baby ribs.
4. Combine the liquid smoke and water together in a mixing bowl. Whisk well until well combined and pour it into the liner pan.
5. Place the spice rubbed baby rib slabs on the 1-inch rack.
6. Set your NuWave oven to the '5' setting and grill your baby ribs for about 90 minutes.
7. Carefully open the dome of the oven, taking care so that you do not burn yourself, and turn the ribs over using metal tongs.
8. Continue grilling the baby ribs for another 3 to 3 and half hours.
9. Once the ribs are done, remove the ribs from the oven and rest for about 10 minutes.
10. Serve hot with a side of grilled vegetables and mashed potatoes.
11. Enjoy!

Brine Soaked And Bacon Covered Grilled Pork Loin

Serves: 2 – 3

Ingredients for the Brine:
- 4 cups water
- 1 tablespoons maple syrup
- 3 tablespoons kosher salt
- 1/4 teaspoon crushed black peppercorns
- 1 large garlic clove, smashed
- 1 sprig fresh sage
- 1 bay leaf

Ingredients for Pork:
- 1 (2 – 2 ¼ pound) pork loin roast, boneless and fat trimmed
- 1 tablespoon finely chopped fresh sage
- 2 garlic cloves, finely chopped
- 2 tablespoons maple syrup, divided
- 1/2 tablespoon cider vinegar
- 8 bacon slices (about 1/2 pound)

Directions:
1. Pour the water for the brine in a medium sized saucepan and heat on a high flame until the water is lightly bubbling.
2. Add in the salt and maple syrup and lower the heat to a medium low. Simmer for a few minutes.
3. Sprinkle the crushed black peppercorns and add in the crushed garlic clove, sprig of fresh sage and the bay leaf in the water.
4. Heat on a high flame and let the water boil for about 2 more minutes.
5. Pour the prepared brine into a deep 3-quart pot. Leave it uncovered and let the brine cool down to room temperature.
6. Place the pork loin in the cooled brine and cover with a lid. Place the covered pot in the refrigerator and leave it in for at least 8 hours or for a maximum period of 24 hours.
7. Combine the garlic, ½ tablespoon syrup and sage together in a small mixing bowl.
8. Pour the spice rub mix over the pork.
9. Arrange the bacon slices over the spice rub covered pork loin in a crossed design. Tuck the loose ends of the bacon under the pork loin.
10. Carefully place the brine soaked and bacon covered pork loin on a 1-inch rack.
11. Grill on the 'HI' setting for about 40 minutes, flipping the pork loin over around the 20-minute mark.
12. While the pork loin roasts in the oven, pour the remaining syrup and vinegar in a small mixing bowl. Whisk well until well combined.
13. Use a pastry brush to lightly brush the prepared vinegar mix over the pork loin and continue roasting on the 'HI' setting for an additional 15 minutes.
14. Once the pork is cooked to perfection, remove the pork loin from the oven and allow it rest for about 15 to 20 minutes before slicing the pork.
15. Slice the pork into thick slices and serve hot with the condiment of your choice.
16. Enjoy!

Tangy Orange Marmalade Glazed Spareribs

Serves: 2

- 1/2 rack pork spare ribs
- 1 teaspoon Dijon mustard
- 1/2 cup orange marmalade, melted
- 1/2 teaspoon lemon juice
- Salt, to taste
- 1/2 tablespoon Worcestershire sauce
- Freshly ground black pepper, to taste

Directions:
1. Spoon the marmalade into a small mixing bowl and leave it out at room temperature in order to melt it. This process should take about 30 to 45 minutes.
2. Add the mustard, Worcestershire sauce and lemon juice to the melted orange marmalade. Whisk well until well combined.
3. Pour the prepared glaze over the spare ribs and spread the glaze evenly all over the spare ribs.
4. Place the glaze covered spare ribs on a 3-inch rack.
5. Set your NuWave oven on the 'HI' setting and grill the spare ribs for about 20 to 25 minutes on each side.
6. Once the timer is up, let the spare ribs rest within the dome for another 5 to 10 minutes before removing them from the oven.
7. Sprinkle salt and pepper over the spare ribs according to your taste.
8. Serve hot.
9. Enjoy!

Hot and Spicy Pork Chops

Serves: 2

Ingredients:
- 2 (1-inch) loin pork chops
- 1 clove garlic, minced
- 3 tablespoons extra virgin olive oil
- 1/2 teaspoon oregano
- 3/4 teaspoons salt
- 1/2 teaspoon cumin
- 1 tablespoon chili powder
- 1 tablespoon fresh cilantro
- 1 tablespoon green chilies

Directions:
1. Pour the extra virgin olive oil into a small mixing bowl.
2. Add in the minced garlic, oregano, salt, cumin, chili powder, fresh cilantro and green chilies to the oil and whisk well.
3. Place the pork chops in a shallow baking dish and pour the prepared herb and seasoning oil over the pork chops.
4. Cover the shallow baking dish with a cling wrap and refrigerate for at least 6 to 8 hours.
5. Place the marinated pork chops in a single layer on a 3-inch rack.
6. Set your NuWave oven on the 'HI' setting and grill for about 12 to 14 minutes per side (increase the cooking time to about 16 to 18 minutes per side if you are using frozen pork chops).
7. Once the pork chops are done, remove them from the oven and let them rest for about 10 minutes before slicing.
8. Serve hot with an accompaniment of your choice.
9. Enjoy!

Fennel and Anise Seed Crusted Pork Loin

Serves: 4

Ingredients:
- Kosher salt, to taste
- 1 tablespoon fennel seeds, crushed
- Freshly ground pepper, to taste
- 1/2 tablespoon anise seeds, crushed
- 1/2 tablespoon olive oil
- 1/2 teaspoon crushed red pepper flakes
- 1 (¾ pound) pork loin

Directions:
1. Combine the salt, fennel seeds, freshly ground black pepper, anise seeds and crushed red pepper flakes together in a small mixing bowl.
2. Pour in the olive oil and mix well to prepare a spiced oil
3. Place the pork loin in a shallow baking dish.
4. Pour the spiced oil over the pork loin and turn it over a few times to ensure that the pork loin is well coated.
5. Cover the baking dish with a plastic wrap and refrigerate for about 4 to 5 hour.
6. Remove the pork loin from the marinade and shake it well to get rid of the excess marinade.
7. Place the marinated pork loin on the 3-inch rack.
8. Set your NuWave oven on the 'HI' setting and grill the pork loin for about 11 to 13 minutes per side.
9. Once the internal temperature of the pork reads 145 degrees Fahrenheit, the pork is done.
10. Remove the done pork loin from the oven and place on the cutting board.
11. Allow the pork loin to rest for about 10 minutes before slicing.
12. Serve hot with the accompaniments of your choice.
13. Enjoy!

Delicious Rum Soaked Pork Chops

Serves: 4 – 6

Ingredients:
- 6 double cut bone-in pork chops
- 4 tablespoons balsamic vinegar
- 1 cup dark rum
- 1/2 cup brown sugar
- 2 teaspoons red chili flakes
- 2 tablespoons chili powder
- 4 teaspoons kosher salt
- 4 tablespoons butter, melted
- 2 teaspoons black pepper

Directions:
1. Place the pork chops in a single layer in the bottom of a shallow baking dish. Keep aside.
2. Pour the balsamic vinegar and dark rum in a medium mixing bowl. Whisk well until well combined.
3. Add in the brown sugar, red chili flakes, red chili powder, kosher salt, butter and black pepper. Continue whisking until all the ingredients are well incorporated.
4. Pour the prepared marinade over the pork chops placed in the baking dish.
5. Set aside to marinate for about 1 hour, turning the chops over every 15 minutes.
6. Remove the pork chops from the marinade and shake off the extra marinade.
7. Place the drained pork chops on a 3-inch rack.
8. Set your oven on the 'HI' setting and bake the pork chops for about 10 minutes per side.
9. Once the pork chops are done, remove them from the oven and let them rest for about 5 minutes before slicing.
10. Serve hot with the accompaniment of your choice.
11. Enjoy!

Beef and Lamb Recipes

Quick and Easy Rib Roast

Serves: 3 – 4

Ingredients:
- 1 (2 ½ pound) standing rib roast, thawed
- 1/2 teaspoon kosher salt
- 1/2 teaspoon onion powder
- 1/2 teaspoon black pepper

Directions:
1. Combine the kosher salt, onion powder and black pepper together in a small mixing bowl.
2. Place the standing rib roast on a cutting board.
3. Sprinkle the prepared rub over the rib roast and rub it in using your fingers. Make sure you rub the spice rub in especially around the boney areas.
4. Place the spice rub coated rib roast on a 1-inch rack with its rib side down.
5. Grill on the 'HI' setting for about 14 to 16 minutes per pound of ribs, for rare done ribs.
6. Remove the ribs from the oven and rest them for about 10 minutes before slicing.
7. Serve hot with hot sauce or barbeque sauce on the side.
8. Enjoy!

Tips:
1. For medium rare done ribs, cook the ribs for about 18 to 20 minutes per pound of ribs.
2. For medium cooked ribs, cook the ribs for about 22 to 24 minutes per pound of ribs.
3. For well-done ribs, cook the ribs for about 28 to 30 minutes (or more) per pound of ribs.

Speedy Lamb Meatballs

Makes: 3 (3 ounce) meatballs

Ingredients:
- 1/2 pound ground lamb
- ¼ teaspoon ground cinnamon
- 2 tablespoons finely chopped scallions
- 1/2 teaspoon ground cumin
- 1/2 teaspoon salt
- 1/2 teaspoon ground allspice
- 1/2 egg, beaten
- 1 1/2 tablespoons semolina

Directions:
1. Place the ground lamb and scallions together in a large mixing bowl. Mix well until well combined.
2. Add in the cinnamon, allspice, semolina, cumin and salt to the meat and scallion mix.
3. Pour the beaten egg over the spice-covered meat and use your hands to lightly knead until you get a semi solid mix. Keep a bowl of cold water handy and constantly wet your palms. This will ensure that the meat doesn't get too sticky to work with.
4. Cover the bowl with a plastic wrap and refrigerate for about an hour or until the meat is firm enough to retain its shape.
5. Divide the meat mixture into 3 parts (about 3 ounces each).
6. Apply oil on your palms and shape each meat portion into a round meatball.
7. Place the meatballs on a 3-inch rack and grill on the 'HI' setting for about 20 to 25 minutes. Pause the oven around the 12-minute mark and turn the meatballs over.
8. Once the meatballs are done, serve hot over a bed of pasta, topped with the sauce of your choice.
9. Enjoy!

Delicious and Cheesy Beef Burgers

Serves: 2

Ingredients:
- 1/2 pound lean ground beef
- 1/2 egg, beaten
- 1/2 tablespoon Worcestershire sauce
- 1/4 cup dry breadcrumbs
- 2 hamburger buns
- 1/4 package dry onion soup mix
- 2 slices American cheese

Directions:
1. In a large mixing bowl, place the ground beef.
2. Pour in the beaten egg and Worcestershire sauce.
3. Add in the onion mix and breadcrumbs.
4. Dampen your hands with cold water and lightly mix until all the ingredients are well incorporated. Do not over mix or else your burger patties will be extremely tough.
5. Divide the prepared meat into 2 equal halves.
6. Lightly dampen your hands and shape the meat portions into two round patties, about ¼ of an-inch thick.
7. Place the prepared beef patties on the 3-inch rack and cook on the 'HI' setting for about 6 to 8 minutes on each side or for about 11 to 13 minutes on each side if you are using frozen patties.
8. Cover the cooked patties with a slice of cheese and cook for another minute or until the cheese melts.
9. Slice the hamburger buns horizontally and place the cheese covered burger patties on the base of the hamburger buns.
10. Cover with condiments of your choice such as lettuce, tomato slices, onion slices, pickle, spiced mayonnaise, mustard, etc.
11. Cover with the top of the bun.
12. Serve hot.
13. Enjoy!

Delicious Ancho Chili Spiced Lamb Burgers

Serves: 3

Sauce Ingredients:
- 1/2 cup ground ancho chili powder,
- 1/2 tablespoon sour cream
- 1/2 cup water
- 2 tablespoons extra-virgin olive oil
- 1 – 1 1/2 tablespoons fresh lime juice
- 1 small clove garlic, chopped
- Black pepper, to taste
- 1/4 tablespoon salt

Burger Ingredients:
- 1 pound grass-fed ground lamb
- 1/4 teaspoon cumin seeds
- 1/4 teaspoon coriander seeds
- 1/4 teaspoon cayenne powder
- Salt, to taste
- 1 clove minced fresh garlic
- 3/4 teaspoons whole black pepper
- 1 1/2 ounces Cotija cheese
- 3 Ciabatta buns
- Red onion, sliced
- Lettuce or spring green mix
- Tomato, sliced

To Prepare The Sauce:
1. Pour the water into a small saucepan and heat over a medium high flame. Add in the ancho chili powder and continue heating until the water is lightly bubbling.
2. Continue heating until about 1/8th of the total liquid remains.
3. Pour the prepared thickened ancho chili liquid into the jar of a blender.
4. Add in the sour cream, garlic, olive oil and lime juice and blitz until smooth.
5. Season to taste with salt and pepper and keep aside.

To Prepare The Burgers:
1. Place the lamb, coriander, cayenne, salt, pepper, cumin, garlic and pepper together in a large mixing bowl. Mix well until all the ingredients are well incorporated.
2. Divide the mixture into 3 equal parts.
3. Lightly dampen your hands with cold water and form one burger patty from each portion.
4. Place the burger patties on the 3-inch rack. Grill on the 'HI' setting for about 7 to 9 minutes per side.
5. Cut the burger buns horizontally. Spread about a teaspoon of the prepared sauce on the bottom bun.
6. Place the grilled burger patty on the sauce and top with lettuce, onion slices, tomato slices and Cotija cheese.
7. Cover with the top half of the bun and serve hot with a side of crisp French fries.
8. Enjoy!

Yankee Style Pot Roast

Serves: 2 – 3

Ingredients:
- 1 ¼ - 1 1/2 pounds shoulder or chuck roast
- 2 large carrots, cut on bias
- 2 large potatoes, cleaned and peeled into quarters
- 1/2 large onion, cut in wedges
- 1/2 teaspoon black pepper
- 1 - 2 sprigs rosemary
- ¼ cup red wine
- 1/2 teaspoon salt
- 1/2 teaspoon pepper

Directions:
1. In a large oven-roasting bag, place the carrots, potatoes and onion together.
2. Place the chuck or shoulder roast over the layer of vegetables.
3. Combine the wine, pepper, salt and rosemary together in a small mixing bowl.
4. Pour the seasoning over the meat.
5. Seal the bag with the tie and make a tiny slit on the top.
6. Place the sealed oven-roasting bag on a 1-inch rack with the side with the slit facing up.
7. Set the oven on the '7' setting and roast for about 4 to 5 hours.
8. Remove the oven-roasting bag from the oven and place on a tray.
9. Rest the meat for about 5 minutes before cutting open the bag.
10. Slice the roasted meat and serve hot topped with the cooking jus and with the roasted vegetables on the side.
11. Enjoy!

Lamb Chops with a Mint and Red Pepper Sauce

Serves: 2

Ingredients:
- 2 (1-inch thick) trimmed shoulder lamb chops
- Coarse salt, to taste
- 1/2 tablespoon dried Italian herbs
- Freshly ground black pepper, to taste
- 1/2 tablespoon olive oil
- 1 1/2 tablespoons fresh lemon juice
- 1 teaspoon Dijon mustard
- 1/4 cup chopped fresh mint
- 3 tablespoons finely chopped red bell pepper

Directions:
1. Combine he coarse sea salt, dried Italian herbs and black pepper together in a small mixing bowl.
2. Pour the prepared spice rub over the lamb chops and lightly rub until the lamb chops are well coated with the spice rub.
3. Place the spice covered lamb chops on a 3-inch rack.
4. Grill the lamb chops on the 'HI' setting for about 5 to 7 minutes on each side.
5. While the lamb chops cook in the oven, place the olive oil, fresh lemon juice, Dijon mustard, fresh mint and red bell pepper together in a small mixing bowl.
6. Whisk using a wire whisk until well combined.
7. Rest the lamb chops for a few minutes before serving.
8. Serve hot, topped with the prepared mint and pepper sauce.
9. Enjoy!

Delicious Andouille & Beef Burgers with Spicy Mayonnaise and Caramelized Onions

Serves: 3

Ingredients:
- 1/4 pound Andouille sausage, cut into ¼-inch cubes
- 1/2 cup pecans, toasted and chopped
- 1/4 pound ground 20% fat beef chuck or ground beef
- 1/2 teaspoon salt
- 1/4 pound sweet onion
- ¼ teaspoon black pepper
- 1 1/2 tablespoons extra virgin olive oil, divided
- 1/2 teaspoon brown sugar
- 1 1/2 tablespoons garlic cloves, minced
- 1/2 cup mayonnaise
- 1/2 teaspoon Cajun or Creole seasoning blend
- 1/2 tablespoon fresh lemon juice
- ¼ teaspoon hot pepper sauce

Directions:
1. Place the Andouille sausage, beef, salt, toasted pecans and black pepper together in a large mixing bowl. Mix well using your hands, until all the ingredients are well incorporated.
2. Lightly dampen your hands and divide the mixture into 3 parts. Shape each part into a ½-inch patty each.
3. Place the burger patties in a flat plate and cover with a plastic wrap. Refrigerate while you prepare rest of the ingredients.
4. Place the sweet onion, garlic, 1-tablespoon olive oil and brown sugar together in the bottom of the liner pan.
5. Pop the liner pan into your NuWave oven and roast the onion mixture on the 'HI' setting for about 12 to 15 minutes.
6. Remove the sweet onion mixture from the liner pan and set aside. Make sure you keep the sweet onion mixture warm.
7. Place the burger patties on the 3-inch rack in a single layer.
8. Grill on the 'HI' setting for about 7 to 9 minutes on each side.
9. While the burgers are cooking in the oven, combine together the mayonnaise, Creole seasoning, ½ tablespoon olive oil, lemon juice and hot pepper sauce together in a small mixing bowl. Cover with a plastic wrap and refrigerate until you need to use it.
10. Slice the hamburger buns horizontally into halves.
11. Place the grilled burger patty on the bottom half of the bun. Spoon the caramelized onions over the burger patty and spoon the spicy mayonnaise over the caramelized onions.
12. Cover with the top half of the hamburger buns.
13. Serve hot with a side of crisp French fries.
14. Enjoy!

Feta and Tomato Topped Grilled Lamb Chops

Serves: 2

Ingredients:
- 1 tablespoon olive oil
- 1/2 tablespoon lemon juice
- 1/2 clove garlic
- 2 (1-inch) lamb chops
- 2 tablespoons chopped ripe tomatoes
- 2 ounces Feta cheese, crumbled
- 2 - 3 Kalamata olives, pitted
- Salt, to taste
- 1/2 tablespoon parsley, chopped
- Freshly ground black pepper, to taste

Directions:
1. Combine the olive oil, lemon juice and garlic together in a shallow dish.
2. Place the lamb chops in the marinade and turn the lamb chops over and over until all the sides of lamb chops are well coated.
3. Cover the dish with plastic wrap and refrigerate for about 15 to 30 minutes.
4. In another small mixing bowl, combine the Feta, olives, tomato and parsley together. Keep aside.
5. Place the marinated lamb chops on the 3-inch rack. Season with salt and pepper.
6. Grill on the 'HI' setting for about 10 to 12 minutes. Flip the lamb chops over around the 5-minute mark.
7. When timer is up, divide the feta mix into two portions.
8. Top each lamb chop with a portion of the prepared feta cheese mix.
9. Grill on the 'HI' setting for another 3 to 5 minutes or until the cheese melts.
10. Serve hot with a side of your favorite accompaniments.
11. Enjoy!

Spicy Louisiana Sliders with a Mustard Remoulade Sauce

Serves: 4

Ingredients for the Remoulade Sauce:
- 1/4 cup mayonnaise
- 2 tablespoons whole-grain mustard
- 2 tablespoons Dijon mustard
- 1 1/2 tablespoons hot sauce
- 1 scallions, finely diced
- 1 1/2 gherkins, finely diced
- Freshly ground black pepper, to taste
- Kosher salt, to taste

Ingredients for the Burgers:
- 1/2 teaspoon sweet paprika
- 1/4 teaspoon garlic powder
- 1/2 teaspoon dried thyme
- 1/4 teaspoon onion powder
- 1 tablespoon salt
- 1/4 teaspoon cayenne pepper
- 3/4 pounds ground beef chuck
- 1 tablespoon black pepper
- 1/2 tablespoon canola oil
- 4 slider buns, split and lightly toasted
- 8 thin slices pepper jack cheese
- 4 sliced red onion
- 1 tablespoon hot sauce
- 4 slices Tasso ham, grilled until golden brown

Directions:
1. Place the mayonnaise, whole grained mustard, Dijon mustard and hot sauce together in a small mixing bowl. Whisk well until all the ingredients are well incorporated.
2. Add in the scallions and gherkins and mix well. Season well with salt and pepper.
3. Cover the bowl with the sauce with a plastic wrap and refrigerate for about an hour before serving.
4. Combine the sweet paprika, garlic powder, dried thyme, onion powder, salt, cayenne pepper and black pepper together in a small mixing bowl.
5. Lightly dampen your hands and divide the ground beef into 4 parts. Shape each part into a patty and make a light indention in the center of the patty.
6. Spoon about $1/4^{th}$ of the prepared spice rub on the top of a patty. Lightly rub it in using your fingers. Make sure you do not disturb the shape of the patty.
7. Repeat with the remaining patties.
8. Place the spic rubbed patties on a 3-inch rack with the spiced sides facing down.
9. Sprinkle salt and pepper over the tops of the patties.
10. Grill on the 'HI' setting for about 7 to 8 minutes on each side.
11. Place two sliced of cheese on each patty and continue grilling for another 2 to 3 minutes in the oven or until the cheese melts.
12. To assemble the burgers, place the grilled patties on the lower halves of the buns.
13. Spread the prepared Remoulade sauce on the patties and top with the sliced onions, ham slices and pour some hot sauce over them.
14. Serve with a side of crisp French fries.
15. Enjoy!

Herb Butter Stuffed Lamb Chops

Yield: 3 lamb chops

Ingredients:
- 3 (2-inch) lamb chops
- 2 cloves garlic, minced
- 1/2 stick soft, unsalted butter
- 1/2 tablespoon fresh parsley, chopped
- 1/2 large shallot, chopped
- 1/2 tablespoon fresh tarragon, chopped
- 1/2 teaspoon salt
- ¼ teaspoon ground black pepper

Directions:
1. Place the garlic, parsley, shallots, tarragon, pepper and salt together in a small mixing bowl. Mix lightly until combined.
2. Add in the butter and whisk until all the ingredients are well incorporated.
3. Place the lamb chops on a plastic wrap covered cutting board. Cover with another sheet of plastic wrap and lightly hammer the lamb chops with a meat tenderizer until flattened about ½-inch thick.
4. Spoon equal amounts of the prepared herb butter onto the lamb chops.
5. Roll the lamb chops and secure into place using toothpicks.
6. Place the prepared stuffed lamb chops on a 3-inch rack.
7. Grill on the 'HI' setting for about 10 to 12 minutes on each side for medium rare done lamb chops. Adjust the cooking time according to your preference.
8. Once done, remove the lamb chops from the oven and rest for about 5 minutes.
9. Serve hot with a side of hot sauce.
10. Enjoy!

Delicious Beef Burger in Olive Bread Slices

Serves: 2

Ingredients:
- 2 tablespoons extra-virgin olive oil, divided
- 2 cloves garlic, crushed
- 5 slices olive bread, toasted
- 1/2 tablespoon sherry vinegar or red wine vinegar
- 2 tablespoons sliced almonds
- 1/4 cup chopped roasted red peppers
- 1/2 teaspoon smoked paprika, divided
- 3/4 pounds ground beef chuck or ground lamb
- 3/4 teaspoon kosher salt, divided
- 1 shallot, finely grated (about 2 tablespoons)
- Lettuce leaves
- 2 slices Manchego cheese

Directions:
1. Take about 1 tablespoon of olive oil and lightly brush the olive bread with it.
2. Line a 3-inch rack with foil and place 1 slice of the olive oil coated olive bread on it, along with the sliced almonds and garlic.
3. Toast the ingredients on the 'HI' setting for about 5 minutes on each side.
4. Extract all the ingredients from the rack. Carefully slice the crust of the bread and discard.
5. Place the toasted bread, almond slices and garlic together in the jar of a blender or food processor. Make sure you tear the bread into small pieces before placing it in the jar of the blender or food processor.
6. Add in the peppers, the remaining 1 tablespoon olive oil, about 1/8 teaspoon salt, vinegar and ¼ teaspoon paprika.
7. Blitz until the mix is slightly chunky.
8. Place the ground meat in a large mixing bowl. Add in the shallots, the remaining ½ teaspoon of kosher salt and the leftover ¼ teaspoon of paprika.
9. Lightly dampen your hands and mix the beef until all the ingredients are well incorporated.
10. Dampen your hands again and divide the beef mixture into two parts. Shape each portion into a burger patty that is about 1-inch thick.
11. Place the prepared burger patties on the 3-inch rack.
12. Grill for about 7 to 10 minutes on each side on the 'HI' setting.
13. Once the timer is up, place the cheese slices on each patty and continue grilling for an additional 2 to 3 minutes or until the cheese melts.
14. Spoon the prepared roasted pepper sauce equally onto the remaining 4 olive oil coated olive bread slices.
15. Place the cheese-topped patties on the roasted pepper sauce and top with lettuce.
16. Serve hot with a side of crisp French fries.
17. Enjoy!

Barbeque Lamb Skewers

Serves: 2

Ingredients
- 1 pound leg of lamb, fat trimmed and cut into 2-inch cubes
- 1/2 red onion, quartered
- 1/2 large green bell pepper, cored and cut into 4 equal pieces
- 4 large white mushrooms
- Barbeque sauce
- 2 Roma tomatoes, cut in half and seeded

Directions:
1. Divide the lamb cubes, onion quarters and green pepper pieces into two equal portions.
2. Thread the lamb cubes, onion quarters, green pepper pieces, mushrooms and Roma tomatoes on to bamboo or metal skewers in an alternating pattern of meat and vegetables.
3. Place the prepared skewers on the 3-inch rack and lightly brush the barbeque sauce over them.
4. Grill on the high setting for about 12 to 15 minutes.
5. Flip the skewers over and again brush them with the barbeque sauce.
6. Continue grilling for another 8 to 10 minutes.
7. Serve hot with barbeque sauce on the side.
8. Enjoy!

Tips:
1. You can also add in some chunks of cottage cheese or tofu to the mix.
2. Grill a few pieces of corn on the cob along with the skewers for a delicious accompaniment.

Delicious Veggie and Meat Tortilla Rolls

Serves: 1

Ingredients:
- 15 ounces meat of your choice (pork, flank steak or chicken)
- 1/2 green pepper
- 1 medium Spanish onion
- 1/2 red pepper
- 1/2 package fajita or taco seasoning mix
- 1/2 yellow pepper
- 4 ounces shredded Cheddar or Mexican cheese
- 4 ounces ready-made salsa mix
- 1/2 package ready-made tortillas
- Pepper, to taste
- Salt, to taste

Directions:
1. Slice the meat, green pepper, Spanish onion, red pepper and yellow pepper into 2 slices about ¼-inch thick each.
2. Sprinkle the taco or fajitas seasoning mix on the meat strips and toss well until well coated.
3. Arrange the vegetables on the outside of a 3-inch rack while placing the meat strips towards the inside.
4. Cook on the 'HI' setting for about 12 to 17 minutes per side if using pork, about 7 to 9 minutes on each side for medium doneness if using flank steak and for about 8 to minutes on each side if using chicken.
5. Place the tortillas in a foil and carefully seal the foil shut.
6. Carefully place the aluminum wrapped tortillas in the liner pan when you open the dome to slip your meats and vegetables over.
7. Once the meat is done cooking, remove the meat and vegetables from the oven.
8. Cautiously unwrap the tortillas from the aluminum foil, making sure that you don't burn yourself.
9. Place the grilled vegetables in a single layer over the warmed tortillas. Layer the cooked meat over the vegetables.
10. Sprinkle a layer of cheese over the meat and top with salsa.
11. Roll the tortillas lightly and serve hot with a salad on the side.
12. Enjoy!

Seafood Recipes

Tasty Tuna Noodle Casserole

Serve: 4-6

Ingredients:
- 1 (5-ounce) can tuna, drained
- 1/2 (10½-ounce) can cream of mushroom soup
- 1 cup egg noodles, cooked
- 1/4 cup water
- 1/4 cup sour cream
- 1/2 cup frozen peas or green beans, thawed
- 2 tablespoons breadcrumbs
- 1/2 cup Cheddar cheese, shredded and divided

Directions:
1. Place the tuna, sour cream, green beans or peas, about 6 tablespoons cheese, cream of mushroom soup, and cooked noodles together in a medium mixing bowl.
2. Mix well until it forms a cohesive mixture.
3. Pour the prepared mix into an 8-inch ovenproof dish.
4. Place the ovenproof dish on the 1-inch rack and cook on the 'HI' setting for about 18 to 22 minutes.
5. Once the timer is up, add the remaining cheese and breadcrumbs on the top of the semi set casserole.
6. Bake on the 'HI' setting for another 2 to 3 minutes or until the cheese melts and gets light brown.
7. Once done, remove the casserole from the oven and cool for about 7 to 10 minutes before serving.
8. Serve hot.
9. Enjoy!

A Medley of Shellfish

Serves: 1

Ingredients:
- 2 littleneck clams
- 2 mussels
- 2 large shrimp
- 1 squid, cleaned and cut into 1-inch rings
- 1 tablespoon olive oil
- 1 clove garlic, minced
- 1/2 tablespoon hot sauce
- 2 tablespoons clam juice
- Dash parsley, minced

Directions:
1. Carefully scrub the mussels and clams until clean.
2. Place the clams, mussels, shrimp, squid rings, olive oil, garlic, hot sauce, clam juice and parsley together in an ovenproof baking dish.
3. Place the baking dish on the 3-inch rack and cook on the 'HI' setting for about 12 to 15 minutes or until all the mussels and clams open up.
4. Serve hot.
5. Enjoy!

Tips:
1. About halfway through the cooking process, pause your oven and carefully extract the baking dish from the oven. Shake it well and return to the oven for cooking. This will help to open up the mussels and clams faster.
2. Do not eat any of the unopened mussels and clams.
3. Do not forget to devein the shrimps and remove the 'poo vein'.

Tangy Lemon Salmon Topped With a Sweet and Spicy Mango Salsa

Serves: 2

Ingredients for the Salmon:
- 2 (6-ounce) salmon fillets
- 1/2 tablespoon olive oil
- 1 tablespoon lemon juice
- 1/2 tablespoon grated lemon zest
- 1/4 teaspoon black pepper
- 1 teaspoon Dijon mustard

Ingredients for the Salsa:
- 1/2 ripe mango, peeled and diced
- 2 tablespoons red bell pepper, chopped
- 1 green onion, finely chopped
- 1 tablespoon lime juice
- 1 tablespoon fresh cilantro, chopped

Directions:
1. Combine the lemon juice, lemon zest, and pepper, olive oil and Dijon mustard together in a small mixing bowl. Whisk well using a wire whisk, until all the ingredients are well incorporated.
2. Place the salmon fillets in a shallow baking dish and pour the prepared marinade over them.
3. Cover with a plastic wrap and let the fish marinate in the refrigerator for about 30to 45 minutes.
4. While the fish marinates in the refrigerator, prepare the salsa.
5. Place the mango, red bell pepper, green onion and cilantro together in a mixing bowl. Mix well.
6. Pour the lemon juice over the prepared salsa and let it sit for about 5 to 7 minutes before mixing again.
7. Cover with a plastic wrap and refrigerate until you need to use it.
8. Place the marinated salmon fillets on the 3-inch rack.
9. Cook on the 'HI' setting for about 7 to 9 minutes per side.
10. Serve hot topped with the chilled mango salsa.
11. Enjoy!

NuWave Style Quick N Easy Lobster Thermidor

Serves: 2

Ingredients:
- 2 (4-6 ounce) lobster tail, shell removed and cut into 1-inch pieces
- 4 tablespoons heavy cream
- 4 tablespoons butter
- 4 tablespoons shallot, minced
- Chopped parsley
- 1 teaspoon dry mustard

Directions:
1. Place the lobster tailpieces in an ovenproof dish.
2. Pour the heavy cream and butter over the pieces and mix well.
3. Add in the shallots and parsley and mix lightly until well coated.
4. Sprinkle the dry mustard on the top and mix again.
5. Place the baking dish on the 3-inch rack.
6. Cook on the 'HI' setting for about 12 to 15 minutes.
7. Remove the lobster pieces from the sauce and place on the serving plate.
8. Spoon the remaining sauce on the side.
9. Serve hot.
10. Enjoy!

Zingy Roasted Shrimp with a Herbed Salsa

Serves: 2

Ingredients for the Shrimp
- 3/4 pounds large shrimp, peeled and deveined
- 3 garlic cloves, thinly sliced
- 1 red Serrano pepper, halved lengthwise
- 1 bay leaf
- 1/2 lemon, cut into wedges
- 1/4 cup olive oil

Ingredients for the Herb Salsa:
- 2 tablespoons fresh cilantro, chopped
- 1/2 tablespoon finely grated lemon zest
- 2 tablespoons fresh flat-leaf parsley, chopped
- 1/2 tablespoon olive oil
- Freshly ground pepper, to taste
- Kosher salt, to taste

Directions:
1. Place the shrimp and Serrano pepper halves in an ovenproof dish, along with the bay leaf, garlic and olive oil.
2. Mix lightly until all the ingredients are coated with olive oil.
3. Place the baking dish on the 3-inch rack.
4. Cook on the 'HI' setting for about 3 to 5 minutes.
5. While the shrimp cooks, prepare the salsa.
6. Combine the cilantro, lemon zest and parsley together in a small mixing bowl.
7. Season to taste with salt and pepper.
8. Pour the olive oil over the salsa and let it stand for a few minutes before mixing it up.
9. When the shrimp is done, pour in the lemon juice and toss well to coat.
10. Serve the shrimp hot, topped with the prepared salsa.
11. Enjoy!

Delicious Potato Topped Tilapia Fillets with A Herbed Sour Cream

Serves: 2

Ingredients:
- 2 tilapia filets
- 1/2 egg
- 1 medium utility potato, peeled & rinsed in water
- 1 tablespoon cornstarch
- Pepper, to taste
- Salt, to taste
- 1/2 cup sour cream
- 1/2 lime, juiced
- 1 bunch fresh dill, finely minced

Directions:
1. Thinly shred the potato and dry on a towel. Press tightly to squeeze the excess water out of the potatoes.
2. Place the dried out potatoes in a small mixing bowl. Add in the cornstarch, beaten egg, salt and pepper. Mix well.
3. Spoon the prepared potato mixture over the tilapia fillets and lightly press.
4. Grease an ovenproof baking dish with some butter or spray with some cooking spray.
5. Place the potato topped tilapia fillets in the greased baking dish. Lightly pour some olive oil over them or spray with some cooking spray.
6. Place the baking dish on a 1-inch rack and cook on the 'HI' setting for about 18 to 20 minutes.
7. While the fish cooks, prepare the dipping sauce.
8. Place the sour cream in a small mixing bowl.
9. Add in dill, salt, lime juice and pepper. Mix well until all the ingredients are well incorporated.
10. When the fish is done remove the fillets from the oven on to a serving plate.
11. Serve hot, topped with a spoonful of the herbed sour cream.
12. Enjoy!

Simple Tuna Steaks with a Tangy Orange Salsa

Serves: 2

Ingredients for the Tuna:
- 2 (5–6-ounce) tuna steaks, ½-inch thick
- 1/2 tablespoon olive oil
- 1/4 teaspoon ground cumin
- 1/4 teaspoon black pepper
- 1/4 teaspoon salt

Ingredients for the Salsa:
- 1/2 teaspoon orange peel, finely shredded
- 1/2 large tomato, seeded and chopped
- 2 medium oranges, peeled, sectioned, and coarsely chopped
- 2 tablespoons fresh cilantro, snipped
- 1 tablespoon walnuts, chopped and toasted
- 1 tablespoon green onion, chopped
- 1/2 tablespoon lime juice
- ¼ teaspoon black pepper
- ¼ teaspoon salt

Directions:
1. Place the cumin, pepper and salt together in a small mixing bowl. Mix well to combine.
2. Use a pastry brush to lightly oil the fish fillets and sprinkle the prepared cumin mixture onto the fillets.
3. Place the spiced fish fillets on a 3-inch rack.
4. Cook on the 'HI' setting for about 5 to 7 minutes per side or until the fish flakes easily when forked.
5. While the fish is cooking, prepare the orange salsa.
6. Place the tomato, coarsely chopped oranges, fresh cilantro, orange peel, walnuts and green onion together in a bowl. Mix well to combine.
7. Season the salsa with salt and pepper.
8. Pour the lemon juice over the salsa and let it sit for about 3 to 4 minutes.
9. Toss well until the salsa is well coated with the lemon juice.
10. Once the fish is done, transfer it to a serving plate and serve hot, topped with the prepared orange salsa.
11. Enjoy!

Spicy Red Snapper with Red Onion and Orange

Serves: 2

Ingredients:
- 2 red snapper filets
- 1 teaspoon garlic, minced
- 2 tablespoons olive oil
- 1/2 tablespoon dark chili powder
- 1/2 red onion, small, sliced thin
- 1/2 orange, sliced
- 4 sprigs thyme
- 1 teaspoon black pepper
- 1/2 tablespoon kosher salt

Directions:
1. Combine the olive oil, chili powder, pepper, garlic and salt together in a bowl. Mix well to forma smooth paste. Keep aside.
2. Place the snapper fillets on a cutting board with the skin side down. Spoon the prepared paste on the flesh side of each fillet and lightly rub it in.
3. Place the orange slices in the bottom of an airtight container in a single layer.
4. Top with a layer of red onion slices.
5. Sprinkle the thyme over it.
6. Place the red snapper fillets and seal the container.
7. Refrigerate for about 2 to 3 hours.
8. Place the red snapper fillets in a single layer on the 3-inch rack.
9. Top with a layer of red onions and orange slices (about 2 of each on each red snapper fillet).
10. Cook on the 'HI' setting for about 6 to 8 minutes on each side.
11. Remove the red snapper fillets from the oven and place on a serving plate.
12. Serve hot, topped with the grilled red onion and orange slices.
13. Enjoy!

Cheesy Crab Dip with Toasted Wonton Wrappers

Serves: 4

Ingredients:
- 1/2 (12-ounce) package 2-inch wonton wrappers, halved diagonally
- 4 ounces cream cheese, brought to room temperature
- Olive oil, to taste
- 2 tablespoons mayonnaise
- 6 ounces lump crab meat
- 2 tablespoons sour cream
- 1/2 cup shredded Cheddar cheese, divided
- 2 green onions, thinly sliced
- 2 tablespoons freshly grated Parmesan cheese
- 1/2 teaspoon Worcestershire sauce
- 1/2 teaspoon sesame oil
- 1/2 teaspoon soy sauce
- 1/4 teaspoon Sriracha (optional)
- Kosher salt, to taste
- 1/4 teaspoon garlic powder
- Freshly ground black pepper, to taste

Directions:
1. Place the wonton wrapper halves in a flat plate. Drizzle the olive oil over them and toss well until well coated.
2. Spread the oil coated wonton wrappers in a single layer on a 3-inch rack.
3. Cook on the 'HI' setting for about 3 to 5 minutes on each side. Take care that the wonton wrappers do not burn.
4. Remove the toasted wanton wrappers from the oven and transfer them to a serving bowl to keep them warm.
5. Spray an ovenproof 10-inch baking dish with some cooking spray.
6. Place the cream cheese, sour cream and mayonnaise together in a large mixing bowl.
7. Whisk well until well combined.
8. Add in the crab meat, ¼ cup Cheddar cheese, green onions, soy sauce, Sriracha, Parmesan, Worcestershire sauce, garlic powder and sesame oil. Mix well.
9. Season to taste with salt and pepper and mix well.
10. Transfer the prepared crabmeat mixture to the prepared baking dish and top with the remaining Cheddar cheese.
11. Place the baking dish on a 3-inch rack.
12. Cook on the 'HI' setting for about 15 to 17 minutes or until the cheese melts and lightly browns.
13. Serve hot with the warm toasted wonton wrappers.
14. Enjoy!

Grilled Halibut with a Tangy Clementine Gremolata

Serves: 8

Ingredients:
- 6 Clementines
- 4 garlic cloves, peeled and minced
- 2/3 cup chopped fresh Italian parsley
- 2 teaspoons sea salt
- 8 (6-ounce) halibut filets
- 1/2 cup extra-virgin olive oil
- Black pepper, to taste

Directions:
1. Remove the peels of the clementines and place the flesh of the fruit in a small bowl.
2. Add in the sea salt, garlic and parsley and mix well until combined.
3. Add in the olive oil and let it stand for about 5 minutes.
4. Mix well and cover the bowl with a plastic wrap. Refrigerate for about an hour or until you need to use the Gremolata.
5. Rub the salt and pepper over the halibut filets and place the halibut fillets on a 1-inch rack.
6. Cook on the 'HI' setting for about 15 to 17 minutes. Flip the halibut fillets over around the 8-minute mark.
7. Check if the fish is done by flaking it with a fork.
8. If done, transfer the halibut fillets to a serving plate and serve hot topped with the chilled clementine Gremolata.
9. Enjoy!

Fennel Coated Bass

Serves: 2

Ingredients:
- 12 ounces stripped or black bass, about 1-inch thick
- 2 tablespoons olive oil
- 2 teaspoons fennel seeds, crushed
- 2 tablespoons lemon juice
- Pepper, to taste
- Salt, to taste

Directions:
1. In a small mixing bowl, combine together the olive oil, salt, fennel, lemon juice and pepper together. Mix well until well combined.
2. Divide the black or stripped bass fillet into two equal portions.
3. Place the bass fillets on a 3-inch rack and spoon the prepared fennel mixture onto the bass fillets.
4. Cook on the 'HI' setting for about 10 to 12 minutes or until the fish easily flakes when struck with a fork.
5. Serve hot with a salad of your choice on the side.
6. Enjoy!

Hot & Zingy Clams & Sausage

Serves: 2

Ingredients:
- 2 sausages, crumbled
- 2 cloves garlic, minced
- 16 littleneck clams, cleaned
- Chopped cilantro, to taste
- Hot sauce, to taste
- Lemon slices as needed

Directions:
1. Place the sausage and clams together in a large mixing bowl.
2. Add in the cilantro, garlic and hot sauce to the bowl.
3. Toss until all the ingredients are well coated.
4. Arrange the clam and sausage mix in the bottom of the liner pan.
5. Cook on the 'HI' setting for about 12 to 15 minutes or until the sausage is cooked and the mussels open up.
6. Serve hot, topped with lemon slices.
7. Enjoy!

Vegetables Recipes

Delicious Mayonnaise & Cheese Covered Corn

Serves: 4 – 8

Ingredients:
- 4 ears of corn, cut into about 4 pieces each
- 1/2 cup mayonnaise
- 1/2 cup melted butter
- 1 cup Queso or Cotija cheese
- Chili powder or paprika, to taste
- Fresco, grated
- Salt, to taste
- 16 lime wedges (optional)
- Pepper, to taste

Directions:
1. Place the corncob pieces on the 3-inch rack.
2. Grill on the 'HI' setting for about 8 to 10 minutes on each side.
3. Remove the corncobs from the oven and immediately pour the butter on each piece of corn.
4. Pour the mayonnaise on the corn.
5. Sprinkle the cheese, salt, chili powder and pepper over the mayonnaise covered corn pieces.
6. Serve hot with lime wedges on the side.
7. Enjoy!

Almond Topped Crunchy French Beans

Serves: 3 – 4

Ingredients:
- 6 ounces French green beans, trimmed and rinsed
- 2 tablespoons lemon juice
- 1 tablespoon olive oil
- ¼ cup almonds, sliced
- 1/2 cup crispy fried onion ringlets
- 1 tablespoon butter, melted

Directions:
1. Place the French beans in an ovenproof 8-inches by 8-inches baking dish.
2. Pour the lemon juice and olive oil over the French beans and place the baking dish on the 1-inch rack.
3. Cook on the 'HI' setting for about 10 to 12 minutes.
4. Sprinkle the almonds and onions over the beans and continue cooking for another 4 to 5 minutes on the 'HI' setting.
5. Remove from the oven and serve immediately.
6. Enjoy!

Cheesy Zucchini and Onion Au Gratin

Serves: 1 – 2

Ingredients:
- 1/2 large yellow onion, cut into ½-inch pieces
- 1/2 tablespoon olive oil
- 1/2 medium zucchini, cut into ½-inch slices
- 1/4 cup Cheddar cheese, shredded
- Pepper, to taste
- Salt, to taste

Directions:
1. Place the yellow onion in a single layer in the liner pan and pour in the olive oil. Toss well.
2. Cook on the 'HI' setting for about 13 to 15 minutes. Around the 8-minute mark, toss the onions around.
3. Place the zucchini slices in a single layer over the grilled onions.
4. Sprinkle salt and pepper to taste.
5. Return the liner pan to the oven and cook on the 'HI' setting for another 5 to 7 minutes.
6. Sprinkle the cheese over the zucchini and cook for an extra 2 to 3 minutes or until the cheese melts.
7. Serve hot.
8. Enjoy!

Parmesan Crusted Asparagus Spears with Balsamic Vinegar

Serves: 3

Ingredients:
- 1/2 pound asparagus
- 1/2 ounce Parmesan cheese, shaved
- 1/2 tablespoon extra-virgin olive oil
- 2 tablespoons balsamic vinegar
- Black pepper, to taste

Directions:
1. Rinse the asparagus well and trim its ends.
2. Pour the olive oil over the asparagus spears and toss well until well coated.
3. Spread the oil coated asparagus on the 3-inch rack in a single layer.
4. Sprinkle the cheese over the asparagus and cook on the 'HI' setting for about 8 to 10 minutes.
5. Remove the Parmesan crusted asparagus spears on to a serving plate.
6. Pour the balsamic vinegar over the asparagus.
7. Serve immediately.
8. Enjoy!

Streusel Topped Buttery Sweet Potato Casserole

Serves: 2 – 3

Ingredients:
- 2 sweet potatoes
- 1/4 cup sugar
- 2/3 cup and 2 tablespoons butter
- 1/4 cup brown sugar
- 1/4 teaspoon salt
- 1 egg, slightly beaten
- 1/2 teaspoon vanilla
- 2 tablespoons pecans, chopped
- 6 teaspoons and 1 teaspoon flour

Directions:
1. Lightly fork the sweet potatoes and place them on a 3-inch rack.
2. Cook on the 'HI' setting for about 40 to 45 minutes.
3. Remove the sweet potatoes from the oven and cool for about 15 to 20 minutes.
4. Once cool enough to handle, peel the sweet potatoes.
5. Place the sweet potatoes in a medium sized bowl and mash into a smooth pulp.
6. Add in the 2/3-cup butter, egg, vanilla, sugar, salt and 1 teaspoon flour. Mix well until all the ingredients are well incorporated.
7. Pour the mixture into a 1-quart ovenproof casserole dish.
8. Place the casserole dish on the 1-inch rack.
9. Cook on the 'HI' setting for about 22 to 25 minutes.
10. While the casserole bakes, combine the remaining flour, leftover butter, pecans and brown sugar together in a mixing bowl.
11. Mix well until combined.
12. Once the timer is up, remove the dome and stir the casserole.
13. Pour the prepared streusel mix over the casserole in an even layer.
14. Continue baking on the 'HI' setting for another 12 to 15 minutes.
15. Serve hot.
16. Enjoy!

Delicious Feta and Artichoke Tortilla Wraps with a Chive and Yogurt Dip

Yields: 12 Rolls

Ingredients:
- 1/2 (14-ounce) can artichoke hearts, drained and chopped finely
- 2 green onions, thinly chopped
- 1/4 cup cream cheese
- 2/3 cup Parmesan or Romano cheese, grated
- 2 tablespoons pesto
- 2 tablespoons Feta cheese, crumbled
- 4 whole tortillas (8-inch)
- 1/2 (8-ounce) carton plain fat-free yogurt
- 1/2 (7-ounce) jar of sweet peppers, water drained and cut vertically
- 1/2 tablespoon chives, roughly chopped

Directions:
1. Grease an 8-inches by 8-inch silicone baking dish with some butter or spray it with some cooking spray. Keep aside.
2. Place the artichoke hearts, green onions, Feta cheese, cream cheese, Parmesan cheese and pesto together in a large mixing bowl. Mix well until well combined.
3. Place about 2 tablespoons of this mix on each tortilla.
4. Top the cream cheese mixture with red pepper strips.
5. Roll the tortilla into a tight roll.
6. Place the tortilla rolls in the prepared silicon-baking dish. Spray lightly with some cooking spray.
7. Place the tortilla filled baking dish on a 3-inch cooking rack.
8. Cook on the 'HI' setting for about 12 to 15 minutes or until the tortillas are thoroughly heated.
9. While the tortilla rolls heat through, prepare the sipping sauce.
10. Combine the chives and yogurt together in a small mixing bowl. Keep aside.
11. Once cooked thoroughly, cut the rolls in 3 parts and place on a serving plate.
12. Serve hot with the chive and yogurt sauce on the side.
13. Enjoy!

Tofu, Cheese and Marinara Sauce Stuffed Bell Peppers

Serves: 2

Ingredients:
- 1/2 cup brown rice
- 1 cup marinara sauce, divided
- 1/2 (12-ounce) tofu, drained and diced
- Salt, to taste
- 2 bell peppers, ¼ tops cut off and seeds removed
- Pepper, to taste
- 4 (½-inch) slices tomato
- 1 cup Mozzarella cheese, shredded and divided

Directions:
1. Follow the instructions on the package and cook the brown rice.
2. Place the peppers in a baking dish.
3. Spoon about ¼ cup of brown rice into each bell pepper.
4. Spoon about ½ cup of the marinara sauce over the layer of the brown rice and top with about 1/4- cup mozzarella cheese each.
5. Divide the tofu equally between the two bell peppers and place over the layer of mozzarella cheese.
6. Place one slice of tomato on each bell pepper.
7. Sprinkle the remaining cheese over the bell peppers.
8. Cover the baking dish with a sheet of aluminum foil and bake on the 'HI' setting for about 18 to 20 minutes.
9. Remove the aluminum sheet and bake for another 3 to 4 minutes on the 'HI' setting.
10. Serve hot with a side of your favorite condiment.
11. Enjoy!

Spicy Grilled Vegetables with a Yogurt and Tahini Dip

Serves: 2

Ingredients:
- 1/2 cup plain fat-free Greek-style yogurt
- 1/2 tablespoon fresh lemon juice
- 3/4 tablespoons tahini
- 1/4 teaspoon ground cumin
- 1/4 teaspoon salt, divided
- 1/2 teaspoon garlic, minced
- 2 tablespoons olive oil
- 6 large button mushrooms
- 1/4 teaspoon Spanish smoked paprika
- 1 tomato, halved horizontally
- 1/2 head of radicchio, quartered
- 1 (3/4 pound) eggplant, cut lengthwise into 4 wedges
- 1/2 medium onion, quartered
- Fresh parsley, chopped (optional)
- ¼ teaspoon black pepper
- 2 Kaiser Rolls

Directions:
1. Combine the yogurt, lemon juice, garlic, tahini, cumin and ¼ teaspoon salt together in a mixing bowl. Whisk using a wire whisk until well combined. Cover with a plastic wrap and refrigerate.
2. In another bowl, pour the oil and add in the paprika. Whisk well until well combined.
3. Place the mushrooms, eggplant, onion, tomato and radicchio together in a bowl.
4. Pour the prepared paprika oil over the vegetables and toss well until well coated.
5. Spread the paprika oil coated vegetables on the 1-inch rack in a single layer.
6. Grill on the 'HI' setting for about 20 to 22 minutes.
7. Around the 10-minute mark, open the dome and mix the vegetables around a bit.
8. Spoon the grilled vegetables on to a serving plate and serve hot with a side of the prepared yogurt and tahini sauce and Kaiser rolls.
9. Enjoy!

Roasted Garlic Mushrooms

Serves: 2

Ingredients:
- 1 (8-ounce) package crimini or button mushrooms, quartered
- 2 cloves garlic, finely chopped
- 2 tablespoon olive oil
- 1 tablespoon fresh thyme, chopped
- Freshly ground black pepper, to taste
- Salt, to taste

Directions:
1. Place the olive oil, garlic and fresh thyme together in a small mixing bowl. Whisk well until well combined.
2. Season to taste with salt and pepper.
3. Pour the marinade over the mushrooms and toss well until the mushrooms are well coated.
4. Place the marinated mushrooms directly onto the liner pan.
5. Roast on the 'HI' setting for about 20 to 25 minutes.
6. Serve hot.
7. Enjoy!

Roasted Cauliflower, Olives and Chickpeas

Serves: 2 – 3

Ingredients:
- 3 cups cauliflower florets
- 4 cloves garlic, coarsely chopped
- 1/2 cup Spanish green olives, pitted
- 1/2 (15-ounce) can chickpeas, rinsed and drained
- 1/4 teaspoon crushed red pepper
- 1 1/2 tablespoons olive oil
- 1 1/2 tablespoons fresh flat leaf parsley
- ¼ teaspoon salt

Directions:
1. Place the cauliflower florets, garlic, Spanish green olives, chickpeas, crushed red pepper, parsley and salt together in a large mixing bowl.
2. Pour the olive oil over the ingredients and let it stand for about 2 to 3 minutes.
3. Toss until all the ingredients are well coated in the olive oil.
4. Place the olive oil coated ingredients in the bottom of a liner pan in a single even layer.
5. Cook on the 'HI' setting for about 22 to 24 minutes.
6. Serve hot with your preferred condiment on the side.
7. Enjoy!

Quick and Easy Roasted Butternut Squash

Serves: 2

Ingredients:
- 1/2 butternut squash, cut in half lengthwise and seeds removed
- 1 teaspoon salt
- 1 teaspoon sugar
- Extra-virgin olive oil, as needed

Directions:
1. Prepare the squash as per the instructions and keep aside.
2. Pour the olive oil over the squash.
3. Combine the sugar and salt together and rub it over the butternut squash half.
4. Place the butternut squash half on a 1-inch rack.
5. Cook on the 'HI' setting for about 35 to 45 minutes.
6. Chop the roasted squash into cubes.
7. Transfer the roasted squash cubes onto a serving plate.
8. Serve hot, topped with some olive oil for garnish.
9. Enjoy!

Delicious Ricotta and Spinach Stuffer Lasagna Rolls

Serves: 2 – 3

Ingredients:
- 4 lasagna noodles, cooked and drained
- 1 clove garlic, minced
- 1/2 medium onion, finely chopped
- 1/2 tablespoon butter
- 1/2 teaspoon oregano
- 1 1/2 cups tomato sauce
- 1/4 teaspoon thyme leaves
- 2 tablespoons mushrooms, chopped (optional)
- 1/4 teaspoon basil
- 1 (5 ounce) package frozen chopped spinach
- 1 tablespoon Parmesan cheese
- 1/2 cup Ricotta or cottage cheese
- Dash black pepper

Directions:
1. Follow the instructions on the package and cook the noodles according to the instructions.
2. Heat the butter in a saucepan and add in the garlic and onion.
3. Sauté for a few minutes until the onion turns translucent and the garlic is aromatic.
4. Pour in the tomato sauce and mix well.
5. Add in the oregano, thyme leave and basil. Mix well and cook for 1 minute.
6. Add in the mushrooms and let the sauce simmer for about 8 to 10 minutes or until the sauce starts to bubble.
7. Take the sauce off the heat and keep it aside.
8. Follow the instructions on the package and cook the spinach. Drain the water from the spinach and squeeze until all the excess water is drained.
9. Place the spinach, pepper, Ricotta (or cottage cheese) and Parmesan cheese together in the jar of a blender. Blitz until smooth.
10. Spoon the mixture onto the end of a lasagna noodle.
11. Roll the noodle tightly to contain the filling in.
12. Repeat with the rest of the lasagna noodles.
13. Place the lasagna noodle rolls in a liner pan that has been sprayed with cooking spray.
14. Pour the prepared sauce over the lasagna noodle rolls.
15. Cook on the 'HI' setting for about 20 to 25 minutes or until the noodle rolls are heated through.
16. Serve hot.
17. Enjoy!

Desserts Recipes

Pumpkin Cookie Sandwiches with a Cream Cheese Filling

Yields: 12 cookies

Ingredients:
- 1/2 cup vegetable oil
- 1 large egg
- 1 cup light brown sugar
- 1/2 cup pumpkin puree
- 1/2 tablespoon pumpkin pie spice
- 1/2 teaspoon vanilla extract
- 1/2 teaspoon baking powder
- 1/2 teaspoon salt
- 1 1/2 cups all-purpose flour
- 1/2 teaspoon baking soda

Cream Cheese Filling Ingredients:
- 1 (4 ounce package) cream cheese, softened
- 2 1/4 cups powdered sugar
- 1/2 cup butter, softened
- 1 teaspoon pure vanilla extract

Directions to Make the Cookies:
1. Grease the liner pan with some butter or spray it with some cooking spray.
2. Place the brown sugar and olive oil together in a bowl. Beat with an electronic beater until smooth.
3. Add in the egg and continue beating until the egg is well incorporated into the mix.
4. Add in the pumpkin puree, vanilla, baking soda, pumpkin pie spice, baking powder and salt. Continue whisking until it gets a light and fluffy texture.
5. Slowly fold using a silicon or rubber spatula. Do not over mix or the batter will fall flat.

6. Use a small cookie spoon or a round tablespoon and scoop the batter onto the greased liner pan. Leave about 2-inches of space between two cookies.
7. Place the Extender Ring on the base of your NuWave oven and cover with the dome.
8. Cook on the 'HI' setting for about 13 to 15 minutes or until the cookies spring back when touched lightly.
9. Let the cookies cool completely before filling them with the cream cheese filling.

Directions to Make the Cream Cheese Filling:
1. Place the cream cheese and butter in the bowl of an electric mixer.
2. Cream the butter and cream cheese together on the medium speed. Stop the mixer at regular interval so that you can scrape the sides of the bowl.
3. Add in the vanilla and continue whisking for another few minutes.
4. Lower the speed of the electric mixer and gradually add in the powdered sugar to the cream cheese and butter mix.
5. Continue beating until the mix is light and fluffy.
6. Spoon the cream cheese filling on the flat side of the cooled cookies. Top with another cookie and press down lightly to make a sandwich.
7. Serve immediately.
8. Enjoy!

Tip:
If you do not have pumpkin pie spice mix handy, use the following recipe to make it at home by combining together:

- 3/4 teaspoon cinnamon
- 1/2 teaspoon ginger
- 1/2 teaspoon nutmeg
- ¼ teaspoon allspice

Delicious Dense Pound Cake

Yield: 1 Cake

Ingredients:
- 3 cups all-purpose flour
- ½ teaspoon salt
- ½ teaspoon baking powder
- 1 cup (about 2 sticks) unsalted butter, softened
- 2 teaspoons pure vanilla extract
- 3 cups sugar
- 1 cup heavy cream
- 6 large eggs

Directions:
1. Sift the flour, salt and baking powder together in a sieve and keep aside.
2. Place the butter and sugar together in the bowl of an electrical mixer. Beat on the medium high speed until it gets creamy and fluffy.
3. Pour in the vanilla extract and continue beating for another minute.
4. Add in the eggs, one at a time, and beat well until the egg gets incorporated into the batter before adding in another egg.
5. Slowly add in the flour mix to the electric mixer bowl, alternating with heavy cream. Make sure you start and end with the flour. This ensures that your cake remains moist.
6. Grease a silicon Bundt pan with some butter or spray it with some cooking spray. Lightly flour the pan.
7. Pour the batter into the prepared Bundt pan.
8. Place the batter filled Bundt pan on a 1-inch rack.
9. Place the extender Ring on the base of your NuWave oven.
10. Bake on the '8' setting of your NuWave oven for about 45 to 50 minutes. Do not open the dome of the oven while the cake bakes or else the cake will become hard and dry.
11. Reduce the temperature setting to the '7' mark and still do not open the dome.
12. Once the timer is up, open the dome and insert a skewer in the center of the cake.

13. If the skewer does not come out clean, bake for another 5 minutes, but do not bake for more than 5 minutes.
14. Remove the cake from the oven and cool in the pan for about 15 minutes
15. Invert the cake onto a serving plate and cut into slices.
16. Serve warm topped with some chocolate sauce or marmalade and with a side of ice cream.
17. Enjoy!

Delicious Chocolate Topped Oat Cookies

Yields: 24 Cookies

Ingredients:
- 6 tablespoons quick-cooking oats
- 6 tablespoons granulated sugar
- 6 tablespoons all-purpose flour
- 1/2 teaspoon ground cinnamon
- 6 tablespoons teaspoon chili powder
- 1/4 teaspoon salt
- 1/4 teaspoon baking soda
- 15 tablespoons melted unsalted butter
- 3/4 cups sliced almonds
- 2 tablespoons half and half cream or whole milk
- 1/2 teaspoon pure vanilla extract
- 2 tablespoons light corn syrup
- 2 ounces fine-quality bittersweet chocolate, chopped

Directions:
1. Place the oats, sugar, chili powder, salt, flour, cinnamon and baking soda together in a large mixing bowl. Whisk well until combined.
2. Add in the almonds and keep aside.
3. Combine the half and half (or milk if using), vanilla extract and corn syrup together in another bowl. Whisk until all the ingredients are well combined.
4. Pour the wet ingredients into the dry ingredients gradually. Fold gently to form a smooth, lump free batter.
5. Grease the liner pan with some butter or spray with some cooking spray.
6. Scoop the batter onto the greased liner pan, leaving about 3-inches between two cookies.
7. Bake on the '9' setting of your NuWave oven for about 14 to 15 minutes or until the cookies look dried out and crisp around the edges.
8. Place a wire rack on a parchment sheet. This will ensure that you do not create a large mess when you drizzle the chocolate over the cookies.

9. Gently transfer the cookies to a wire rack and cool to room temperature.
10. While the cookies cool, melt the chocolate over a double boiler of simmering water or microwave for 30-second intervals until the chocolate is completely liquidated.
11. Use a spoon to drip the melted chocolate over the cookies and make a variety of patterns on the cookies.
12. Serve after the chocolate has cooled and solidified.
13. Enjoy!

Lemon And Poppy Seed Glazed Cookies

Yields: 6 cookies

Ingredients to Make the Cookies:
- 1 cup sifted flour
- ¼ teaspoon salt
- ¼ teaspoon baking powder
- 1/4 cup confectioners' sugar
- 1/2 cup (1 stick) unsalted butter

Ingredients to Make the Glaze:
- 1/2 cup confectioners' sugar
- 1/2 tablespoon fresh lemon juice
- 2 tablespoons heavy cream
- 1/2 teaspoon poppy seeds

Directions to Make the Cookies:
1. Sieve the flour, salt and baking powder together in a bowl and keep aside.
2. Place the butter in a small bowl and cream with an electronic beater until light and fluffy.
3. Slowly add the sugar to the butter and continue beating until all the sugar is incorporated and the mix is light in texture.
4. Gradually pour the dry ingredients into the creamed butter mix and continue blending until all the dry ingredients are incorporated into the butter mix.
5. Oil your hands and roll balls about 1-inch balls from the dough.
6. Arrange the balls on a flat cookie sheet in a single layer and refrigerate for about 20 to 25 minutes.
7. Place the dough balls in a single layer on the 1-inch rack and bake on the 'HI' setting for about 12 to 15 minutes.
8. If all the dough balls do not fit on the rack in one go, you might have to bake the cookies in multiple batches.
9. Transfer the baked cookies onto a wire rack and cool to room temperature before glazing.

Directions to Make the Glaze:
1. Place the confectioners' sugar, lemon juice and cream together in a mixing bowl. Whisk until well combined.
2. Add in the poppy seeds and mix well until well incorporated.
3. Once the cookies have cooled, drizzle the prepared glaze over the cookies or dip the top halves of the cookies directly into the glaze.
4. Let the glaze set on the cookies for about 15 to 20 minutes before serving.
5. Enjoy!

Maraschino Cherry Stuffed Cherry Glazed Cookies

Yield: 12 cookies

Ingredients to Make the Cookies:
- 3/4 cups flour
- 1/4 cup unsalted butter, softened
- 1/4 teaspoon salt
- 6 tablespoons powdered sugar
- 1/2 teaspoon vanilla
- 1 tablespoon milk
- 12 maraschino cherries, drained from the liquid, liquid reserved for the glaze and stems removed

Ingredients to Make the Glaze:
- 10 tablespoons powdered sugar, divided
- 1 tablespoon reserved maraschino cherry juice
- 1/2 tablespoon butter, melted

Directions to Make the Cookies:
1. Sieve together the flour and salt in a small bowl. Keep aside.
2. Place the butter and sugar together in another bowl and beat with an electronic beater until fluffy and light.
3. Slowly add in the milk, while continuously beating until the milk is incorporated.
4. Add in the vanilla and continue beating.
5. Slowly add in the flour mix in small increments to the butter and milk mixture. Beat until the flour mix is incorporated into the batter to form a smooth dough.
6. Roll the dough into a smooth log and divide it into 12 equal parts.
7. Oil your hands and roll the portions into a small bowl.
8. Lightly press the center of the ball to flatten it.
9. Place a single maraschino cherry in the venter of the dough.
10. Bring the sides of the cookie up and roll the ball until the cherry is completely covered.

11. Place the cherry center balls around the perimeter of a greased liner pan. Leave about an-inch of space between two cookies.
12. Add the Extender Ring to the base of the NuWave oven.
13. Bake on the '9' setting of your NuWave oven for about 20 to 22 minutes.
14. Once the timer is up, immediately open the dome to release the extra moisture from the oven.
15. Let the cookies cool to a manageable temperature before removing them from the liner pan.
16. Transfer the cookies onto wire rack with parchment paper placed below it.
17. Let the cookies cool completely before glazing them.

Directions to Make the Glaze:
1. Place about 8 tablespoons of the powdered sugar, maraschino cherry juice and butter together in a small mixing bowl.
2. Beat on the medium speed with an electronic beater until the glaze is smooth. Add in more maraschino cherry juice if the glaze is too thick.
3. Dip the top halves of the cookies into the glaze and place them back on the wire rack with the glazed side up.
4. You can also fill a piping bag with the glaze or use a spoon to drizzle the glaze over the cookies.
5. Let the glaze set for 15 to 20 minutes and sprinkle the remaining icing sugar over the cookies.
6. Serve immediately.
7. Enjoy!

Lemon Candy Topped Iced Cookies

Yield: 24 cookies

Ingredients to Make the Cookies:
- 2 cups all-purpose flour (sifted)
- 1/2 teaspoon baking powder
- Salt as per taste
- 1/4 cup (1/2 stick) unsalted butter, softened
- 1 cup granulated sugar
- 1/4 cup shortening
- 1 large egg
- 1 teaspoon pure vanilla extract

Ingredients to Make the Icing:
- 1 cup powdered sugar
- 1 – 2 tablespoons milk
- 1/2 teaspoon vanilla
- 1/3 cup crushed lemon candies

Directions to Make the Cookies:
1. Sieve together the flour, salt and baking powder together in a large mixing bowl and keep aside.
2. Place the shortening, sugar, vanilla, butter and egg together in the bowl of an electric mixer.
3. Beat on a low speed until all the ingredients start getting creamed together.
4. Slowly add in the flour mix, a little at a time, to the butter mix.
5. Continue beating until all the flour in incorporated in and forms a smooth dough.
6. Divide the dough into two equal parts.
7. Cover each part of dough in a plastic wrap and refrigerate for about 6 to 8 hours.
8. When you are ready to bake, remove the refrigerated dough from the fridge and leave it out until it reaches room temperature.

9. Place a plastic wrap on your working station and place the dough on it.
10. Cover with another plastic wrap and roll the dough until it is about 1/8-inch thick
11. Transfer the dough onto a floured working surface. Use a cookie cutter to cut cookies in the shape that you desire.
12. Place the cookies on 1inch intervals on the liner pan.
13. Bake on the '9' setting of your NuWave oven for about 13 to 15 minutes.
14. Once the timer is up, immediately open the dome to release the extra moisture from the oven.
15. Let the cookies cool to a manageable temperature before removing them from the liner pan.
16. Transfer the cookies onto wire rack with parchment paper placed below it.
17. Let the cookies cool completely before glazing them.
18. Repeat with the remaining dough until you have a batch of cookies.

Directions to Make the Icing:
1. Place the milk, powdered sugar and vanilla together in a large bowl.
2. Whisk using a wire whisk and continue beating until the mix is thick enough to spread.
3. Dip the top halves of the cookies into the icing and place them back on the wire rack with the iced side up.
4. You can also fill a piping bag with the icing or use a spoon to drizzle the icing over the cookies.
5. Top with the lemon candies.
6. Serve immediately.
7. Enjoy!

Salted Chocolate Tart

Serves: 5 – 6

Ingredients:
- 1 cup crushed sea salt potato chips
- 3 tablespoons melted unsalted butter
- 2 tablespoons all-purpose flour
- 10 tablespoons heavy cream, divided
- 1/2 teaspoon vanilla extract
- 5 ounces semisweet chocolate morsels
- ¼ teaspoon salt
- 4 ounces bittersweet chocolate morsels
- 1 large egg
- Sea salt for garnish

Directions:
1. Place the crushed sea salt flavored potato chips, flour and melted butter together in the jar of a blender or food processor. Blitz for about a minute until all the ingredients are well combined.
2. Lightly grease a spring form pan with some butter or spray with some cooking spray.
3. Press the prepared chip and melted butter mixture in the bottom and over the sides of the greased spring form pan.
4. Place the spring form pan on a 3-inch rack and bake on the 'HI' setting for about 5 minutes until the crust hardens.
5. Remove the crust from the oven and keep aside until cooled to room temperature.
6. Pour about 2 tablespoons of the heavy whipping cream into a small saucepan. Heat over a medium low flame until the heavy cream is just lightly bubbling.
7. Reduce the flame to a low and add the semisweet chocolate morsels to the cream. Gently mix using a rubber spatula until the chocolate melts and becomes smooth. Take off heat.
8. Add in the salt and vanilla to the chocolate mix. Mix well.

9. Add the eggs one by one to the chocolate mix and mix well until the egg is incorporated, before adding another egg.
10. Pour the prepared salted chocolate mix onto the prepared crust and tap lightly against the kitchen counter to ensure that there are no air bubbles.
11. Place the Extender Ring on the base of your NuWave oven and place the spring form pan on the 1-inch rack.
12. Bake on the '8' setting for about 16 to 18 minutes.
13. Increase the temperature setting to '9' and bake for another 10 minutes.
14. Remove the pan from the oven and cool for a few minutes.
15. While the pie cools, prepare the ganache.
16. Heat the remaining heavy whipping cream on a medium high flame in a saucepan until lightly bubbling.
17. Take the saucepan off the heat and add the bittersweet chocolate morsels to the warm cream.
18. Mix well until smooth.
19. Once the pie is cooled, pour the prepared ganache over it. Use a spatula to make an even layer.
20. Refrigerate for 8 to 10 hours or until overnight.
21. Cut into slices and serve topped with a pinch of sea salt.
22. Enjoy!

Conclusion

The NuWave oven uses revolutionary technology that can easily change the workings of your kitchen! With its energy efficient and time saving technology, you no longer need to spend hours in a hot and stuffy kitchen, slaving over food!

In this book, I have provided you with everything that you need to know about the NuWave oven. This book has the advantage of using a NuWave oven, tips and tricks for quicker and better cooking, FAQs, a brief on all the components and buttons present on the oven, temperature conversions, a handy kitchen conversion guide and a bunch of NuWave recipes for every meal!

I would like to take this opportunity to thank you for purchasing this book and I hope you find the content of this book useful.

Happy Cooking!

CPSIA information can be obtained
at www.ICGtesting.com
Printed in the USA
BVOW09s0831280217
477351BV00003B/45/P